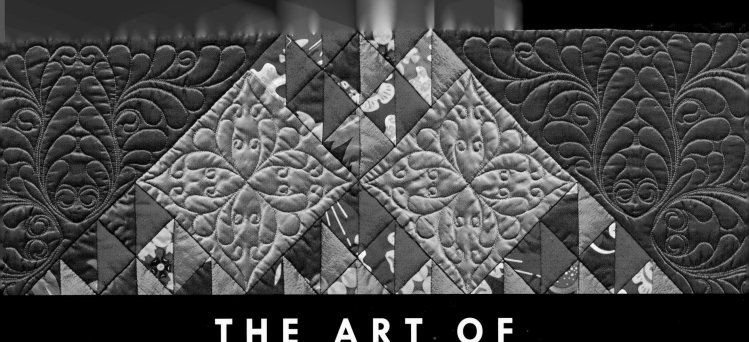

THE ART OF
Mixing Textiles in Quilts

14 Projects Using Wool, Silk, Cotton & Home Decor Fabrics

LYNN SCHMITT *of A Different Box of Crayons*

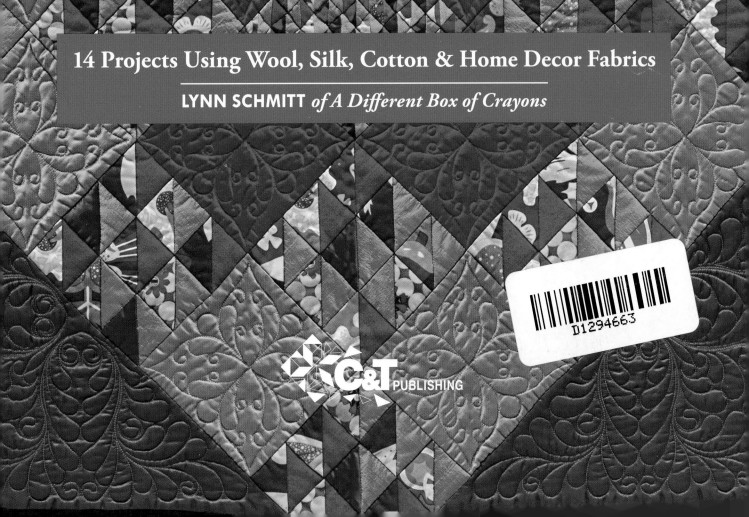

C&T PUBLISHING

Text copyright © 2018 by Lynn Schmitt

Photography and artwork copyright © 2018 by C&T Publishing, Inc.

Publisher: Amy Marson

Creative Director: Gailen Runge

Acquisitions Editor: Roxane Cerda

Managing Editor: Liz Aneloski

Editor: Kathryn Patterson

Technical Editor: Julie Waldman

Cover/Book Designer: April Mostek

Production Coordinator: Zinnia Heinzmann

Production Editor: Jennifer Warren

Illustrator: Aliza Shalit

Photo Assistant: Mai Yong Vang

Style photography by Lucy Glover and instructional photography by Mai Yong Vang of C&T Publishing, Inc., unless otherwise noted

Published by C&T Publishing, Inc., P.O. Box 1456, Lafayette, CA 94549

Library of Congress Cataloging-in-Publication Data

Names: Schmitt, Lynn, 1951- author.

Title: The art of mixing textiles in quilts : 14 projects using wool, silk, cotton & home decor fabrics / Lynn Schmitt of A Different Box of Crayons.

Description: Lafayette, CA : C&T Publishing, Inc., 2018.

Identifiers: LCCN 2017049259 | ISBN 9781617455407 (soft cover)

Subjects: LCSH: Patchwork--Patterns. | Quilting--Patterns.

Classification: LCC TT835 .S3457 2018 | DDC 746.46/041--dc23

LC record available at https://lccn.loc.gov/2017049259

Printed in the USA

10 9 8 7 6 5 4 3 2 1

PROJECTS

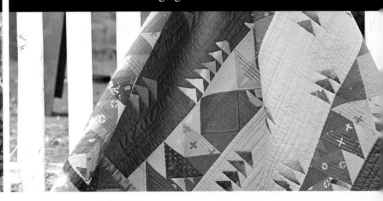

DEDICATION

With overwhelming gratitude, I dedicate this book to all the free spirits I have known in my life, especially those in the quilting community. I thank my mentors, who along the way have guided, encouraged, taught, and molded me, not just in this vocation but also throughout all the manifestations of my careers.

It all naturally started with my parents, without whom there would be no me. To my mother, who gave me that first box of crayons—and oh, glory, the day she bought the 96-count box with the sharpener! To my dad and brother, who taught me by example to work and work and work until it was *right*, not just complete.

To Grandma Elsie, without whom I would never have had the courage to question or even to try to fly.

To my children, Colin and Dana, for the joy and light they shine into my world, and for whom I push on every day, wanting to show them that obstacles are there to be overcome.

To my husband, Gerry, for his love, patience, support, and guidance, especially when things seemed overwhelming and the end was so far out of sight.

Thank you to all of you for believing in me when I sometimes didn't. I am the sum of so many things, and you each bring a color to my crayon box that is unique to you—one I would never want to be without.

ACKNOWLEDGMENTS

My sincere thanks to Dawn Larsen, my internationally award-winning longarm quilter extraordinaire, without whom I would have only half the vision.

A big thank-you to Sue Henderson, my dear friend, without whom none of this would be possible. She remains my right hand and at times my left hand, too, keeping me grounded in so many ways when it is often hard to stay on a single path.

And—last but never least—thank you to Renee Nanneman, my dear friend, co-teacher, and quilting maven. With love and patience, she has taught me, guided me, and held my hand along the way.

Introduction

It may be that you are not yourself luminous, but you are a conductor of light. Some people without possessing genius have a remarkable power of stimulating it.

—Sir Arthur Conan Doyle

"Inspiration—where does it come from?" That's a question I am often asked. The answer isn't as simple as it is concise: Inspiration comes from everywhere.

Design isn't so much an occupation or even a profession for me as it is a way of life. And when I say that, I mean it on a very fundamental, visceral level. It's a way of *seeing*. And feeling, of course, but it all starts with the seeing part, and that itself is more than just perceiving something. It's a process that only just begins with that—the visual encounter of something. That visual experience is the trigger. If the image is powerful, even in some small, subjective way, and the stars are aligned at that moment (okay, maybe I'm being a bit dramatic here, but there *is* a certain unpredictable magic to it), what we often call "inspiration" follows.

I think designers can sometimes be thought of as mediums, channeling a kind of energy wrought from a visual experience and holding it for a moment, just long enough to imbue that energy with form, line, and texture. Only then do they send it on its way, newly clad in color and context, to complete the composition to which this "inspiration" has given birth. We are at

times simply prisms; we accept the raw light of an evocative visual experience and split that light into wavelengths of intense hue to be woven into something new, which hopefully will give others pleasure in experiencing it, too.

So where do I find inspiration? In a world so rich in visual treasure, maybe the better question is where do I *not*? It surrounds us every day. With this book, I hope to inspire you and enable you to open your mind and heart to yet another new facet of our quilting world: mixed-medium textiles. It isn't really a new concept. It's an old one revisited with new eyes. It is not the intent of this volume to discourage you from using cotton—quite the contrary. It is only to ask you to consider *adding* to your cotton world. The possibilities truly are endless, and the hues that different textures of fabrics lend to our palette give a whole new depth to the colors in which we play. Certainly there is much to be learned, but it is mostly common sense (and a lot of trial and error). I've often said, "I make the mistakes, so you don't have to!" and believe me, I have … yet I am not discouraged. I am excited! I know I have only scratched the surface in terms of the possibilities this eclectic textile world holds, and I hope you, too, will enjoy playing with my box of crayons.

Exploring New Textiles:

ECLECTIC FABRIC GUIDELINES

Ode to My Divas Bolster

Ode to My Divas was one of my first patterns designed for use with mixed-medium textiles. I developed it to illustrate the texture and depth of color achieved through the combining of wools, silks, batiks, traditional and non-traditional cottons, and even selectively chosen upholstery fabrics. The look is scrappy and requires only small bits of many things to elevate the project to a rich display of texture and color.

The foundation of "eclectics" is working with alternative textiles within the context of traditional quilting. One of the reasons I was first drawn to quilting was because, as with many other art forms, you can track history within the piece itself. The spirit of the times can be seen in the colors and the degree of playfulness or somberness in the prints. The technology is reflected in what fabrics and fibers were available, the printing and weaving processes that produced them, the fabric dyes by which they were colored, and certainly the techniques used to sew them.

Cotton is a staple and remains the backbone of the quilting industry. But the alternative textures and finishes afforded by silks, wools, linens, and home decor fabrics

open a whole new world of possibilities to today's quilting community. I am not suggesting that cotton be replaced, but it can be enhanced.

Admittedly, I have been referred to by some as the Quilt Heretic for advocating such a seemingly outlandish concept, but the reality is that the concept itself is not new. In the mid-1800s and later into Victorian times it was not uncommon to find silks, wools, tapestries, velvets, and even upholstery fabrics in quilt tops. Think about traditional crazy quilts. They are best known for their glorious embroidery, but they were also constructed with many alternative fabrics, the more sumptuous the better.

One of the explanations I have come across for the origins of crazy quilts includes a kind of neighborhood one-upmanship. It seems that many crazy quilts were created in a round-robin fashion. The quilt was handed from one neighbor to the next, and each in turn would add her fabric and embellishment to the top. Of course, the fabrics the quilters would add would be the best and most beautiful they could afford to share—a bit of velvet here, a silk sash repurposed, or a swatch from the drapes there. The quality of the fabric they added reflected their social status. They incorporated their best, in whatever form that took.

Wool was also often used in quilts, but this was not a function of ego. It was a result of utility; the fabric simply was warmer. It was used in quilt tops and repurposed as batting when the tops wore through.

Today we can blend it all. Cottons can be paired with textiles heretofore considered unsuitable for quilting, or they can stand alone. Silks, wools, textured fabrics, and especially home decor fabrics *can* be incorporated into quilting. Textile considerations for new projects can be expanded beyond color and pattern. Now the sheen and texture of a fabric become new components for consideration when assembling a palette. My desire to expand the possibilities has resulted in considerable experimentation and much trial and error. When it comes to eclectics, I'll say it again: I make the mistakes, so you don't have to!

The guidelines that follow are not meant to represent an all-encompassing document addressing *all* fabric types—but they are a good start, and with this book in hand you will be well on your way to experimenting with alternative types of fabric textures.

A few universal admonitions:

- *Always* test your materials, especially for heat resistance, before beginning any project.

- Due to the multiple finishes and diverse densities of mixed-medium textiles, pinning is always recommended.

- Pressing and consideration of the resulting thickness of the seams is key to the success of an eclectic project.

- Instructions given throughout the projects are often a result of collaboration with my longarm quilter.

- To ensure the best results, press all your fabrics before using them.

- When assigning fabrics to locations in the quilt background, try not to have two heavy fabrics come together (upholstery and wool, two wools, and so on). Avoiding this bulk will make seaming and final

quilting easier and will result in a flatter quilt top. With eclectic fabrics, pressing directions are recommended based on the fabric weights rather than on the traditional light-to-dark rule most often used in quilting. Press *away* from the heavier of the two fabrics regardless of the color. If two heavy fabrics do come together, press the seam open. Try to create opposing seams wherever possible.

- *And most importantly, let go of the quilting rules! We are about to make a whole new set. What a wondrous "box of crayons" you are about to explore.*

Wool

Wool is a textile fiber obtained from sheep and certain other animals, including goats, musk oxen, alpaca, and even Angora rabbits. The wool offered in my Eclectic Bundles and kits, and typically in quilt shops, is wool obtained from sheep.

I feel that the wool most appropriate for quilting is woven, not needle felted. It may be either wet felted or simply wound onto bolts. When you are choosing wool for quilting, the density of the weave is the first element you should consider. Melton, flannel, and worsted are all grades of woven wool readily available.

Wool melton is a thick, heavy, tightly woven fabric with a heavily brushed nap, giving the material a smooth finish with no visible weaving yarns. A medium weight is about as heavy as I would recommend using for piecing. The heavier-weight melton makes for bulkier seams. Worsted wool and wool flannel are lighter weight, have a softer hand, are often used as backgrounds, and can be used easily in piecing.

Most wool can be appropriate in the right application but should be evaluated individually on its ability to be seamed flat. This relates to the density or thickness of the wool.

The density of the weave is greatly affected by whether the wool has been wet felted or not. Wool typically used for piecing is not felted. Wool used for appliqué benefits greatly from the resulting tighter edge obtained during the felting process.

The process of wet felting is simple. Felting occurs when natural fibers, stimulated by friction and lubricated by moisture (usually soapy water), are agitated and rub against one another, in effect making little "tacking" stitches. The process tends to work well with wool fibers because their scales, when aggravated, readily bond together. The result is a tighter weave and a denser fabric with little fraying on the edges when cut. Most wool fabrics can be felted by simply washing them in a hot water bath, agitating, and then shocking the fibers with cold water. Drying in a clothes dryer will shrink the fibers even more. It is important to recognize that when a yard of wool is felted it will reduce in size approximately 20%–30% in *both* directions. The degree of shrinkage depends on the original weave and the fiber content.

Some of the wool you will find in fabric stores sold as yard goods may be blended with synthetic fibers such as nylon or polyester. If you wish to felt these fabrics, make sure the proportion of synthetic fibers is no greater than 20%. The synthetic content will resist felting. Hand-dyed wool, by virtue of the dyeing process, has already been felted. It is usually 100% wool and is regarded as the best wool to work with in quilting, especially for appliqué. Blends may be appropriate for background or piecing elements, but, again, a lower percentage of synthetic content is best.

SEAMING

Wool is by nature a thicker fabric, whether it has been felted or not, and has a looser weave than cotton. Wool will generally stretch more than cotton. To help control this stretch during piecing, shorten your stitch length and use a walking foot. Use a *scant ¼"* seam allowance by stitching just one needle's width shy of the traditional ¼" seam allowance. When feeding fabrics through your sewing machine, place the wool on the machine bed, with the fabric that it is being sewn to on top. Trim the block as you go to keep the dimensions true.

HEAT

Wool has a midrange pressing temperature, which can be aided by steam. Be careful. Wool by its nature absorbs moisture, and too much steam may cause the fabric to stretch. It is usually best to press away from the sewn edge or to press the seams open when piecing. Press from the back using a pressing cloth and finish lightly on the front. A clapper, described in Favorite Things (page 22), is also a great help in pressing seams open.

- A new needle is always a good idea when you are starting a new project. I use a universal or microtex 70 or 80 needle.

- Wool will not usually require a backing of any kind when used for interior piecing. If you are using it for the outer borders, however, and you anticipate that the final quilting will be done on a longarm quilting machine, consider stabilizing the wool border with interfacing. The tension from the longarm frame may stretch the wool. The interfacing will help reduce this stretching.

- When using wool for appliqué, I would use a lightweight interfacing on most weaves (see Wool Appliqué … My Way, page 12).

Silk

Silk is a textile fiber spun by silkworms. The worms spin their fiber around the pupae within their cocoons. The cocoons are then processed, the fibers spun onto spools, and the fabric woven. There are many grades and textures of silk available in the marketplace, and several types of silk are used throughout the projects presented in this book.

Matka is simply defined as raw silk, but there are many grades and finishes. A smooth finish with an expressed weave and matte sheen is what we typically refer to as silk matka. Textured silk matka and even raw silk, which has a heavier, coarser surface and a natural un-dyed appearance, are also used frequently. The shiniest members of the silk family are the silk dupionis and the silk shantungs. Upholstery-weight silks can be either heavily textured or smooth-patterned wovens. The variety is vast, and the fabrics created with this fiber lend such an amazing element of sheen and texture that the effort in using them is well worth the investment of time. The weight and texture of individual fabrics will vary greatly. *Note:* All silk is vulnerable to sun rot and fading. Be sure to keep your finished project out of direct sunlight.

Note: I would not recommend using Indian jacquard silk in quilting projects that will be subject to wear and tear (wallhangings, yes—bed quilts, no). The metallic fibers in many of these types of prints are short and tend to pop out and fray.

SILK MATKA **TEXTURED SILK MATKA**

SILK DUPIONI

PATTERNED SILK DUPIONI **RADIANCE SILK/COTTON BLEND**

SEAMING

Silk is a fine fiber. Most silk fabrics will have a low density or loft, and some may have a loose weave. Finer silk is a lighter texture and is prone to fraying. Do not interpret that to mean that the fiber itself is softer or more fragile than cotton. The reality is that the fiber is stronger than cotton but also finer and smoother. All these factors, especially in dupioni and shantung textures, contribute to the fraying. Coarser silks like silk matka or textured silk matka may be heavier than cotton but are woven more loosely.

The key to success with silk is interfacing. It stabilizes the fibers and reduces the tension on the fabric. Most silks will benefit from a lightweight interfacing. I typically use products like EK130 Easy-Knit or 950F ShirTailor (by Pellon), Touch O'Gold II (by HTC Retail), or Presto Sheer for interfacing silks. Refer to the manufacturer's instructions and apply the interfacing to the wrong side of the silks with a low-heat setting before the fabric is cut. Use a pressing cloth, and try not to slide your iron. A blotting motion works best.

By its nature, silk will tend to slide when sewn, and therefore pinning is strongly recommended. Silk is seamed in much the same manner as cotton, but a shortened stitch length will help hold the looser weaves in place. When seaming silk to other fabrics, place the silk on top as you feed it through your machine so you can make sure it doesn't creep away from the seamline.

TIP • Use a microtex or sharps 80 or 90 needle for best results in sewing silks.

HEAT

Silk requires a low-heat setting, and, like hair, it can be damaged if pressed with too high a temperature. *Always* test your fabric. Press from the back whenever possible. Seams can be pressed in either direction.

Upholstery or Home Decor Fabric

Upholstery fabrics—or *home decor textiles*, as they are referred to in the commercial and home decor industries—is a very generic term that refers to any number of fabrics that have been woven into a construction able to withstand greater abrasion than clothing fabrics or traditional cotton textiles. Exclusive of silk upholstery, for which you can refer to the information on silk, these textiles are typically denser and often have synthetic content. This category of textiles includes jacquards, tapestries, chenilles, velvets, and cotton and linen blends, to name only a few.

When evaluating upholstery fabrics for use in piecing, the weight and fabric content are the most important things to consider. Due to the low melting point of polyester and nylon, a textile blended with a natural fiber like linen or cotton will be easiest to work with. The market, however, does not make natural-fiber home decor goods readily available, nor are they very budget-friendly when you can find them.

Synthetic and semisynthetic fibers you will likely come across include rayon, nylon, polyester, and viscose. Avoid textiles with a synthetic coating on the back. It is there to stabilize the face fibers, and this backing can make it very difficult to press and seam.

Consider both the front and back when evaluating upholstery textiles for use. You may sometimes like the look of the back better than the front and can even take advantage of two coordinated looks by using both sides in one project. With jacquard weaves, where the back may have larger areas of loose "jump" threads, take heed of how and where you plan to use the fabric. Jump threads are vulnerable to being caught or pulled during the final quilting and when the item is in use.

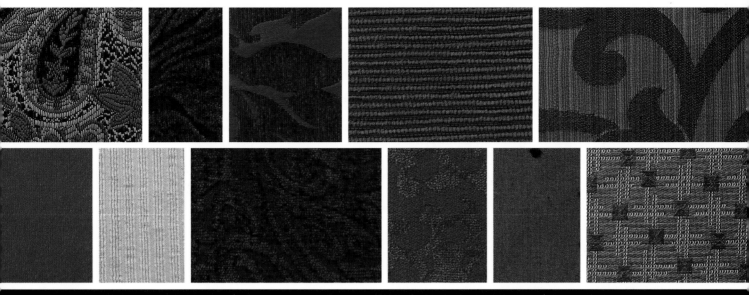

UPHOLSTERY AND HOME DECOR FABRICS

SEAMING

Due to the increased density of upholstery textiles, many of the same techniques for working with wool will apply to how you approach working with home decor and upholstery fabrics. Chenille and velvet, both cut and uncut, have a *nap*, or raised fibers on the surface of the fabric. This nap should be placed on the bed of the machine; the fabric being sewn to the chenille or velvet should be placed on the top. This will help control the slippage and creeping that can result.

Press the seams away from the upholstery textile or, more often, open—whichever is easiest. Do not get caught up in the traditional pressing rules of quilting, which advocate always pressing to one side and toward the darker fabric. Letting the fabric tell you which way to press will help you achieve the flattest possible join. Avoid pressing toward the upholstery textile.

When joining upholstery textiles to adjacent piecing, always pin the intersection points on both sides to create nested seams. This may require clipping into the seam allowance just shy of the sewing line, allowing the seam allowance to turn in the opposite direction from which the rest of the seam is pressed. Nested seams help create flatter and more accurate intersections. Without nested seams, the thickness of upholstery textiles will make accurate intersections very difficult to achieve.

HEAT

The higher the synthetic content of the fabric, the lower the pressing temperature you should use. *Always* test your fabric first. Textiles should be pressed from the back and lightly finished on the face. Fabrics having a nap, like velvet, cut velvet, or chenille, need special care to avoid flattening the nap. Never press these fabrics from the front. Press from the back, with the textile face in a terry towel or a needle board whenever possible. If the nap becomes flattened but isn't melted from excessive heat, it may be possible to revive it with a light spritz of water or steam. Generally, a moderate heat and steam level are best.

TIPS

- The smoother and shinier the face of the fabric, the more challenging it may be to use.

- The sharpest of needles, a new microtex or sharps 80 or 90 needle, is best. Quilting needles can be used for fabrics that are especially dense. More typical textiles will be fine with a universal 75 or 80 needle, but it too should be new.

- If the textile is especially dense or has a heavy nap, consider taking the seam allowances one thread shy of the normal seaming line.

- Consider using interfacing if the weave is loose.

- Fabrics with a nap will benefit from the use of a walking foot on your sewing machine.

Techniques

Wool Appliqué … My Way

Wool appliqué is a raw-edge method of appliqué, and, as with any technique, there are at least two distinct schools of thought on how to execute it. One advocates the use of a double-sided fusible web, both as a pattern transfer and as a means of adhering the wool appliqué to the background. The other calls for using the wool as is and employing freezer paper as a means of transferring the pattern to the wool. Both approaches typically use a decorative edge stitch to finish the appliqué.

There are pros and cons to each method. My experience has been that the fusible web is a good tool to reduce fraying if the wool is loosely woven or the appliqué shapes are small or pointed. Wool that has been well felted typically will not have fraying issues, but loose weaves, even after felting, may still present a problem.

The downside to using fusible web, in my opinion, is that the wool becomes very stiff and flat and is hard to stitch through. The downside to *not* using fusible web is that the edge is more ragged or primitive, and small, clean shapes are difficult to achieve. To a large extent, the decision comes down to personal preference. One technique or the other may better lend itself to the look you are trying to achieve in a given project.

My method falls somewhere in between. It uses a light-weight fusible interfacing (different from fusible web) on all the wool appliqué elements. It is fusible on only one side and remains soft while reducing fraying on the edges of the appliqué pieces. It also gives added loft to the finished appliqué elements. I am often asked what I have placed under the appliqué, and a trapunto application is the expected answer. Simply, there is nothing beneath the fabric except the interfacing. I strive for an invisible edge stitch rather than a pronounced decorative one. Any kind of edge stitch can be used for embellishment if desired, but decorative stitching is not required, as the affixation to the background is virtually invisible.

Here's how to approach wool appliqué … my way:

1. Apply the interfacing to the wrong side of the wool before cutting. (I use a product made by Pellon called EK130 Easy-Knit. It is a nonwoven tricot product.) Follow the manufacturer's instructions for adhering the interfacing. Be sure to use a pressing cloth and a light water spritz for the best adhesion.

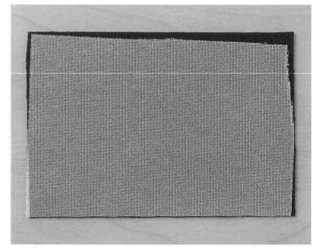

Apply interfacing to back of wool.

2. Trace all the appliqué shapes, in the quantities indicated, onto the matte side of freezer paper. Refer to the pattern photos for color placement.

Trace appliqué pattern.

Note:

- *Full-size right-reading images of all the appliqué shapes are included with each project.*

- *Broken lines on the appliqué patterns indicate the completion of each shape as it would appear beneath the one on top of it.*

- *You may prefer to draw small circle shapes (such as the wool pennies for Bohemian Dance) onto the freezer paper with a circle template rather than using the patterns given.*

3. Using paper scissors, cut out the templates on the lines.

4. Iron the templates to the right side of the prepared wool.

Press to right side of wool.

5. Cut out the wool using sharp, pointed fabric scissors. Follow the edges of the freezer-paper templates and make all your cuts as smooth as possible.

Cut out appliqué piece.

TIP • A good pair of sharp scissors is important. Refer to Favorite Things (page 22) for some great suggestions!

6. Remove the freezer-paper templates. Using a pressing cloth and light water spritz, re-press the cut appliqué pieces from the back. This will tighten the edges of the appliqué pieces and slightly pull back the edges of the interfacing from the edges of the wool.

Back of appliqué before and after second ironing

TIP • The process of appliquéing may cause the background fabric to feel like it has shrunk or shifted. Stitching can do that, depending on the density of the pattern and how careful you are at initially finding the right orientation. Oversizing the background is a great way to compensate for either of these common issues. Mark the general appliqué area with lines of basting stitches or chalk lines showing the block size plus the seam allowances. By making the background piece oversize, you can, if necessary, make any adjustments to the trim line of the background once the appliqué is complete.

7. Fold the background piece in half in both directions to find the center. Gently press the fold lines to make orienting your appliqué work easier.

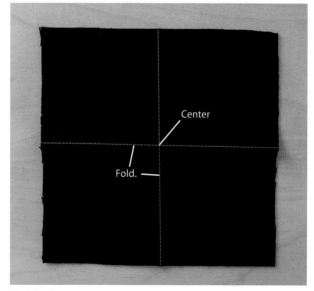

Find background center.

8. Lay out your design on the background, referring to the pattern photographs and images.

Note: The appliqué patterns are all marked with letter codes. These codes refer to the order in which you should appliqué the pieces in place. Appliqué all the elements of the design, working from the background up, as indicated by these codes on the pattern images. First appliqué all the shapes coded with A, then all the B elements, then the C elements, and so on.

9. Secure the pieces to the background one layer at a time, with either small dots of Roxanne Glue-Baste-It (see Favorite Things, page 22) or small appliqué pins.

TIPS

• If you are using Glue-Baste-It, try to avoid gluing in areas where you will be stitching. The glue, although temporary, can be quite hard to stitch through. In addition, use a frugal hand; small dots are plenty to hold a piece in place while you work.

• I invisibly whipstitch my wool appliqué in place using a chenille #24 needle and wool thread. Genziana, Aurifil Lana Wool, and the new Wonderfil Ellana are all great products. Custom-color wool thread kits are available for many of the projects presented here and can be found on my website.

• Cut threads no longer than 18″. This will reduce the chance that the thread will unravel or thin too much while stitching.

• Keep your stitches shallow and perpendicular to the edge of the appliqué for the most invisible results. Wool thread has no sheen and will naturally bury itself in the wool elements. The interfacing applied before cutting will reduce the fraying of the edges and points and give added strength to the weave of the wool, thus allowing you to take very shallow yet secure stitches. Too tight of a stitch will cause the edge to ruffle. Practice will help you achieve the most even and invisible result.

10. Invisibly stitch the appliqué edges in place.

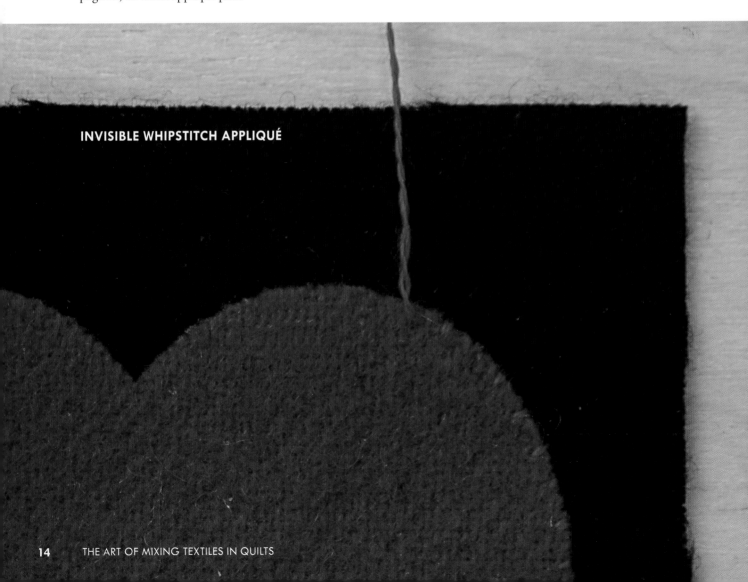

INVISIBLE WHIPSTITCH APPLIQUÉ

COMPLETED WOOL APPLIQUÉ

POINTS

A sometimes-troublesome detail in wool appliqué is handling points. It is the natural tendency of wool to fray when elements of a design are very pointed. You can certainly round off points when cutting, but if you follow the process that follows—along with the addition of the interfacing—you can achieve a very crisp outline.

Assuming you are right-handed, it will seem natural to stitch around an object in a counterclockwise direction while holding the object in your left hand. If you are left-handed, that would be reversed. Remember to take small perpendicular stitches on the surface of the appliqué, traveling (going from one stitch to the next) on the back side of the project and coming up in the appliqué. Stitches should be about ⅛″ or less apart. The appliqué will be secured onto the background with basting glue before you begin to stitch, but the points may still tend to curve away from you as you approach them. These few steps should help in keeping them straight. As you approach a point, follow this order of stitching:

1. As you approach the point, stop stitching ⅛″–¼″ away from the point (A).

2. Secure the opposite edge (B); then come up in the background fabric, just barely beyond the point of the appliqué.

3. Stitch directly into the point using a point-and-stab motion (C).

4. Return to the edge of the appliqué from which you approached the point or corner, and, if necessary, complete the line of stitching. Resume stitching away from the point or corner you have just secured on the opposite side.

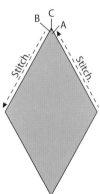

Stitching points

The techniques expanded upon within the pattern instructions are ones that I revert to often in the construction of these projects. That is not to say that these methods are the only ways to accomplish these ends, but they are mine. Experiment with different approaches, and find the ones that best fit you, your tools, and your lifestyle.

Double-Fold Straight-Grain Binding

1. Piece the binding strips together with diagonal seams to make a continuous binding strip. Trim the seam allowance to ¼″. Press the seams open.

Sew.

Sew from corner to corner.

Trim.

Completed diagonal seam—right side

2. Press the entire strip in half lengthwise, with wrong sides together. With the raw edges even, pin the binding to the front edge of the quilt starting a few inches away from a corner, leaving the first few inches of the binding unattached. Start sewing using a ¼″ seam allowance.

---

3. Stop ¼″ away from the first corner (fig. A), and backstitch 1 stitch. Lift the presser foot and needle. Rotate the quilt one-quarter turn. Fold the binding at a right angle so it extends straight above the quilt and the fold forms a 45° angle in the corner (fig. B). Then bring the binding strip down even with the edge of the quilt (fig. C).

4. Begin sewing at the folded edge. Repeat in the same manner at all the corners.

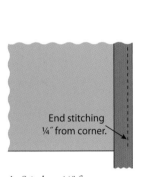

End stitching ¼″ from corner.

A. Stitch to ¼″ from corner.

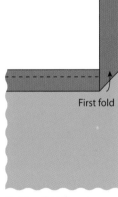

First fold

B. First fold for miter

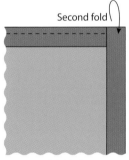

Second fold

C. Second fold alignment

---

5. Continue stitching until you are back near the beginning of the binding strip.

FINISHING THE BINDING ENDS: METHOD ONE

1. After stitching around the quilt, fold under the beginning tail of the binding strip ¼″ so the raw edge will be inside the binding after it is turned to the back of the quilt.

2. Place the end tail of the binding strip over the beginning folded end. Continue to attach the binding, and stitch slightly beyond the starting stitches.

3. Trim the excess binding. Fold the binding over the raw edges to the quilt back and hand stitch, mitering the corners.

FINISHING THE BINDING ENDS: METHOD TWO

1. Fold the ending tail of the binding back on itself where it meets the beginning binding tail. From the fold, measure and mark the cut width of the binding strip. Cut the ending binding tail to this measurement. For example, if your binding is cut 2½″ wide, measure 2½″ from the fold on the ending tail of the binding, and cut the binding tail to this length.

2. Open both tails. Place one tail on top of the other tail at right angles, right sides together. Mark a diagonal line from corner to corner and stitch on the line. Check that the seam has been sewn correctly and that the binding fits the quilt; then trim the seam allowance to ¼″. Press open.

3. Refold the binding, and stitch this binding section in place on the quilt. Fold the binding over the raw edges to the quilt back and hand stitch.

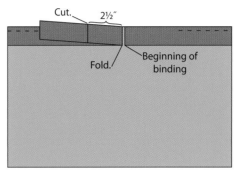

Cut binding tail.

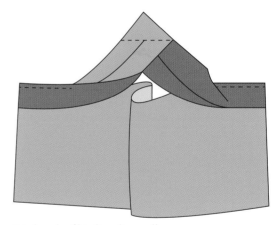

Stitch ends of binding diagonally.

Embroidery

BULLION KNOTS

Bullion knots are used to accent the poppies in Umbrian Fields. Using variegated thread gives an added dimension to the embroidery.

1. To begin the bullion knot, bring the thread up from the back of your work at what will be the top of the stitch, point A. Leaving the thread loose on the face of the fabric, go down at point B (the end of the stitch) and emerge again at point A. Do not pull the needle all the way through to the face.

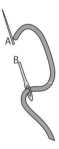

2. Wrap the thread around the point of the needle in a clockwise motion as many times as it takes to cover approximately the same amount of space on the needle as there is space between points A and B. Make the wrapping solid but not too tight.

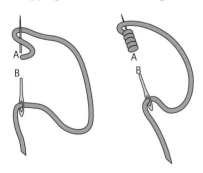

3. Holding the wrapping with your fingers, slowly pull the needle through the wrapped thread and the fabric.

4. Gently lay the wraps back down on the face of the fabric, and pull the needle down again at point B. Adjust the wraps if needed to straighten.

STEM STITCH

A stem stitch is often used as an outline stitch around an appliqué element or as a line of stitching that might represent a stem, for example. It is used in Ode to My Divas for the pistils of the flowers.

1. Using a chalk pencil or removable marker of your choice, draw the line that you would like to stitch onto the background.

2. Knot your thread on the back and come to the surface at point A. Working from left to right, go down at point B and come back up through point C. Continue in the same manner down the entire length of the drawn line.

COUCHING

Couching is a hand embroidery technique that is simply an exposed whipstitch crossing over a yarn or cord at regular intervals, perpendicular to the yarn. Elements can be couched with a matching thread, making the application, especially with yarn, virtually invisible. For added interest, consider couching with a contrasting color or texture of thread. We use alternative textures in textiles—why not extend the concept to thread?

Yarn to be couched is temporarily secured onto the background by placing pins only into the background on either side of the yarn, with the yarn held in place beneath the shafts of the pins.

FRENCH KNOTS

French knots are used as "punctuation," or dots of color and texture, in some of the projects. This embroidery stitch is great for creating texture.

1. Bring the needle straight up from the back of the fabric where you want to place a French knot.

2. Wrap the thread around the needle in a counterclockwise motion 3 or 4 times.

3. Reinsert the needle into the fabric at the same point you emerged, bringing the wraps moderately tight. The looser you leave the wraps, the looser and larger the knot will be on the project surface.

ROSETTE CHAIN STITCH

The rosette chain stitch is used to outline the center medallion elements of the *Echoes of Italy Bolster*.

1. Draw 2 parallel lines with chalk pencil as far apart as you want the width of the stitches to be. For embellishing the appliqué, the top line will be right where the appliqué and background meet, and the bottom line will be on the appliquéd piece. You'll be working from right to left.

Knot the thread and bring your needle up at the top line at point A. Move over about ⅛". Push the needle down at point B and bring it up on the bottom line at point C, but don't pull the needle all the way through the fabric.

2. Bring the thread from right to left over the top of the needle, and wrap it from left to right *under* the needle. Then pull the needle through.

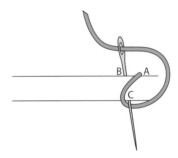

3. Now bring the needle through the right leg at the top line. Pull the thread through gently.

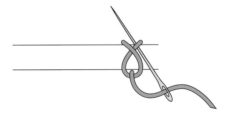

4. Begin the next stitch by moving ⅛" to the left on the top line. End the row of stitches by taking a stitch ⅛" to the left to tack down the last full stitch, and tie off.

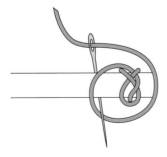

Beading

Beading would take an entire volume in itself to explain adequately, and honestly, I have only begun to explore the possibilities this medium holds. I can say that my approach to it as a "crayon," however, is not just one of embellishment. Certainly, beading can lend that characteristic shimmer we all associate with it, but beads can also create a texture all their own. And they are not even all round! Who knew that seed beads could be peanut shaped or that such things as piggy beads even existed? There is so much to explore. In the *Echoes of Italy Bolster*, I scattered beads in kind of an ombré pattern throughout the appliqué background, changing the density of their placement to sculpt the background of the appliqué.

First, a few basics I have learned. Beads can be added to quilt projects as edge embellishment, background texture, or surface embellishment that takes the place of—or augments—an appliqué detail. They play heavily in the embellishment details of Echoes of Italy.

I use either a beading or sharps #10 needle and Nymo synthetic thread for attachment. When I began adding beads to projects, I initially used a cotton thread but quickly came to understand that not all beads are created equal. Many may have a rough edge around the hole, which is quite capable of cutting typical sewing threads.

In choosing thread, natural or synthetic, two considerations are foremost—visibility and use. Most thread will not be seen, but if you are using transparent beads it may, and the color that reads through is a consideration. Natural thread offers many more beautiful color options than synthetic. Cotton or silk embroidery floss can be used on pieces where the thread shows. If the piece you are beading will be handled, a synthetic thread like Nymo, which is more durable, should be considered. Synthetic thread comes in a variety of sizes; choose the largest thread size that will still fit through the bead you are using.

When working with any thread, cut lengths no longer than 18″–20″. Stretch the thread before you begin beading. Hold a cut thread in both hands and pull from the opposite ends. This will help straighten the thread and make it less likely to tangle when in use. When threading, moisten the eye of the needle, not the thread. If the thread frays or is difficult to insert into the eye, try both ends of the thread and both sides of the needle. The eye of a needle is typically larger on one side than the other because of the way that needles are manufactured.

The traditional stitches, and the simplest ones I have used in beading, are the single bead stitch and the running bead stitch. They are illustrated below.

Single bead stitch

Running bead stitch

The constant in both stitches is that you start with a knot similar to a French knot. Wrap the tail of the thread around the needle several times. Holding the thread wraps on the needle in your hand, pull the needle through. This will create a tight knot at the end of the thread. Come up from the back of the fabric to begin attaching the first bead.

The temptation when sewing on beads is just to string them one to the next in a continuous row without stopping. This can be done, but I advise against it. I have found that, depending on the bead, I often go through a single bead several times before moving on to the next to ensure that it lies flat.

It is also not a bad idea to take a tacking stitch or knot off after 1″ of beading or after five or six bead stitches have been added. This way, if a thread should get cut and a few beads are lost, at least you won't lose the entire beaded length. Knot off the thread by using a typical tacking knot: Take a short stitch on the back side of the fabric in a concealed place. Before tightening the loop of the stitch, go through twice more and tighten.

Favorite Things

When asked to identify my favorite things, I first heard Julie Andrews singing in the background. Upon coming to my senses, I started to contemplate the myriad sewing notions that clutter my studio counters. The writing of this book has caused me to reflect on the items I come back to time and time again when piecing with eclectic textiles. There are some that I truly don't believe I would want to be without. I will attempt to share them here.

First and foremost, there are, of course, my rulers, my rotary cutters, and my two BERNINA sewing machines. The specific models, I think, are individual preferences. They all pretty much do the job.

Sewing Toys

I find it difficult to be without these.

BASTING GLUE: Roxanne Glue-Baste-It is my favorite for wool appliqué. It is a great fixative that provides a temporary bond for the placement and positioning of appliqué shapes.

CIRCLE TEMPLATE: An architectural circle template is a great tool to have for drawing circle appliqués and marking curves.

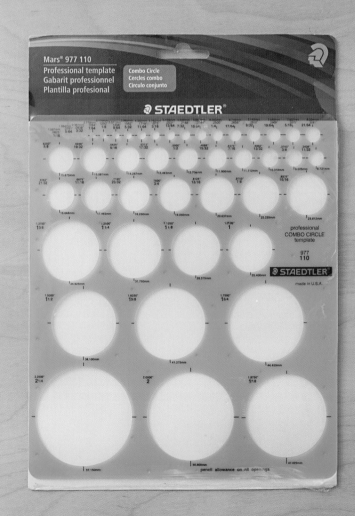

CLAPPER: A clapper, in a quilting context, is not something that turns the lights on and off; it is actually an old tailor's tool used for pressing. A clapper is a thick piece of porous wood that, when applied with moderate pressure to a steamed seam, will help greatly to flatten it. It is a somewhat scientific process involving steam, pressure, and the porous nature of wool. Suffice it to say it works great, and I would not be without it when pressing wool and home decor textile seams. The Steady Betty makes a version of a clapper that achieves the same results.

FUSIBLE INTERFACING: This product makes all things possible when it comes to diverse textiles. It stabilizes the fabric yet doesn't change the fabric's feel, or *hand*. When used with wool appliqué, it also adds to the loft of the quilted shapes. I have experimented with those easiest to find, like Easy-Knit and ShirTailor (both by Pellon) and a new product called Touch O'Gold II (by HTC). Being lightweight and being fusible on *one* side are the deciding factors.

NEEDLES: On this one, the choice is about personal preference and how the needles fit in your hand more than the brand. For wool appliqué work, I prefer a chenille #24 needle, and for heavier specialty threads and embroidery a chenille #22 needle (it has a larger eye and is a bit easier to thread). For beading, a beading needle or straw #10 needle would be the one I seek out.

PINS: When you are seaming textiles of different weights, pinning often helps ensure better joins. Pinning with traditional pins, however, can distort the fabrics. I have found that the extrafine glass-head pins by Clover really work the best in terms of securing the join without moving the fabrics being joined.

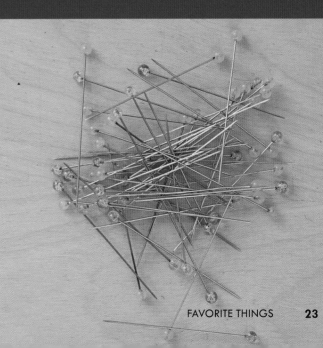

SCISSORS: We all have our favorite scissors, but I must admit that the KAI 5½″ embroidery scissors have become mine for cutting wool appliqué elements. They are extremely sharp and cut an accurate edge. The curved version is nice for cutting circles and curved pieces, and the 6½″ embroidery scissors are invaluable for larger appliqué elements.

STILETTO: A stiletto is a third hand, if you will. It has a long pointed tip, which, among other uses, is a great help in guiding slippery fabrics under the needle when sewing. Silks, silk blends, and fabrics with nap tend to want to creep away from the aligned edges. ByAnnie.com makes a stiletto that I would recommend to all; it has a slightly barbed tip and a flat end at the opposite side for finger-pressing.

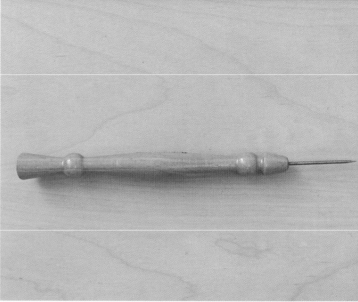

THREADS: Wool thread is a must for wool appliqué! Aurifil Lana Wool and Wonderfil Ellana are my favorites. Wool threads are all by necessity wool and acrylic blends. Although the cost per yard is higher, I recommend the smaller spools when you can acquire them. Handwork does not usually require large quantities of any single thread; more likely, it will require more variety of thread in smaller quantities. Personally, I would rather have more variety of color than greater quantity of unnecessary thread. Matching the color of the thread to the appliqué is the most important deciding factor. The closer the color, the more invisible the stitching.

SPECIALTY THREADS by Wonderfil, especially Eleganza, Razzle, and Dazzle, are my favorites for embellishment. The color and sparkle are outstanding.

Beading requires a slightly tougher thread. I have attached beads in the past using cotton, and initially it was fine. However, beads often have a rough interior edge that is difficult to see, and the result can be that the beads cut the thread once the piece is in use. (And yes … no more beads!) I have found that although the color choices are more limited, Nymo, a synthetic beading thread, is a good answer.

Maintaining Your Tools When Using Eclectic Textiles

• Change your needle as often as possible. I once met a lady who proudly announced she had never changed her needle in twelve years. Please don't let that be you! Change your needle often. The sharper and newer the point, the less likely it is that your silks and fabrics with heavier texture will shatter and pull. A universal needle is fine. The recommended weights for the individual textiles are listed in Exploring New Textiles: Eclectic Fabric Guidelines (page 6). Sharpness is key, and keeping the needle free from barbs becomes even more important when sewing with silks and finer textiles. If possible, change your needle with every new project.

• Clean your machine. Wool sheds a great deal of lint, and if you are not mindful it can accumulate under the throat plate and in the mechanism of your machine. Some home decor fabrics have a similar problem. Anything with a nap will shed.

• A walking foot or even-feed foot will make a great deal of difference in the success of your piecing. Many of these eclectic textiles have looser weaves, and the natural motion of your machine may cause them to stretch. An even-feed foot helps feed them more evenly.

• I use a 45 mm rotary blade in my rotary cutter for these textiles. At times, I may opt for a pinking blade to help reduce the fraying—especially if I am working with silk dupioni. I find the larger rotary blades cumbersome, and the smaller 28 mm blades are just not adequate to cut these heavier textiles. One thing to recognize is that due to the surprising strength of silk fibers, your blade may dull more quickly. Change the blade as needed. A dull blade can negatively impact your accuracy, especially when you are using heavier textiles.

Umbrian Fields

Umbrian Fields Wallhanging

Finished blocks:

Four-Patch: 3″ × 3″ • Pinwheel: 4″ × 4″ • Flying Geese: 1½″ × 3″

Finished wallhanging: 25″ × 25″

Umbrian Fields was one of the first mixed-medium colorways I introduced. Its intent was to illustrate the versatility of the eclectics concept by applying it in a multitude of project types. I created this design after returning from a trip to the Umbrian region of Italy, where one could not help but be inspired by the color and texture of the landscape. There, poppies grow wild in great abundance during late spring and wave in the wind.

These projects are made of simple traditional blocks executed in nontraditional fabrics. Wool, tapestry, raw silk, woven silk, and a vast variety of cottons all found a home in the Umbrian Fields color palette. The project focus is on contrasting textures and my method of executing wool appliqué.

The background for an appliqué project does not always need to be a solid or a single piece of fabric. The background for this project is generally light but has sparks of color and contrasting textures, making it as interesting as the appliqué itself.

Read Exploring New Textiles: Eclectic Fabric Guidelines (page 6) before beginning.

Materials

Fabric requirements are based on a fabric width of at least 40″, except where noted.

FABRICS FOR BORDERS AND BACKGROUND

Brown textured upholstery: ¼ yard for top and bottom borders

Brown chenille dot on green *and* green tapestry print: ⅛ yard *each* for side borders

Assorted light fabrics: ⅜ yard *total* of at least 4 fabrics for background

Green woven wool: 1 fat quarter (18″ × 20″) for background and Pinwheel blocks

FABRICS FOR BLOCKS

Mixed-medium fabrics: ½ yard *total* of at least 7 fabrics for Four-Patch blocks and background squares

Gold cotton print: 1 fat quarter (18″ × 20″) for Pinwheel blocks

Gold cottons: ⅛ yard *each* of 3 fabrics for Flying Geese blocks

Gold upholstery: ⅛ yard for Flying Geese blocks

Brown cotton: 1 fat quarter (18″ × 20″) for Flying Geese blocks

HAND-DYED WOOL FOR APPLIQUÉ

Reds: 3 fabrics, *each* approximately 6″ × 8″, for poppies

Greens: ¼ yard *each* of 2 fabrics (medium and dark) for leaves and pods

Gold: Approximately 4″ × 4″ for poppy details

Black: Approximately 6″ × 6″ for poppy details

OTHER MATERIALS

Interfacing for hand-dyed wools and silk

Green yarn: Approximately 3 yards *each* of 2 different textures for stems

Color-coordinating wool thread for appliqué

Perle cotton #8: Valdani #O521 for details on poppy pods (*optional*)

Backing: ⅞ yard

Binding: ¼ yard

Batting: 28″ × 28″

Cutting

BROWN TEXTURED UPHOLSTERY

• Cut 2 strips 2½″ × 25½″ (A).

BROWN CHENILLE DOT ON GREEN *AND* GREEN TAPESTRY PRINT

• Cut 1 strip 2½″ × 21½″ from *each* fabric (B and C).

ASSORTED LIGHT FABRICS

• From light 1, cut 1 strip 3½″ × 13½″ (E) and 1 strip 3½″ × 5½″ (D).

• From light 2, cut 2 strips 3½″ × 5½″ (G and H) and 1 strip 2½″ × 3½″ (F).

• From light 3, cut 1 strip 3½″ × 18½″ (K) and 1 strip 3½″ × 10½″ (J).

• From light 4, cut 1 strip 3½″ × 10½″ (M) and 1 strip 3½″ × 8½″ (L).

GREEN WOVEN WOOL

• Cut 1 strip 3½″ × 5½″ (N) for the background.

• Cut 6 squares 2⅞″ × 2⅞″ for the Pinwheel blocks.

MIXED-MEDIUM FABRICS

• Cut 15 squares 2½″ × 2½″ for the background.

• Cut 12 squares 2″ × 2″ for the Four-Patch blocks.

GOLD COTTON PRINT

• Cut 6 squares 2⅞″ × 2⅞″.

GOLD COTTONS *AND* GOLD UPHOLSTERY

• Cut 4 strips 2″ × 3½″ from *each* of the 4 golds. (You will have 2 extra.)

BROWN COTTON

• Cut 28 squares 2″ × 2″.

BINDING

• Cut 3 strips 2½″ × width of fabric.

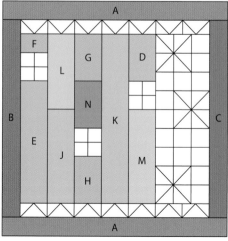

Fabric placement

Construction

All seam allowances are ¼″ unless otherwise noted. Construct all the block elements of the background before joining the columns shown in the wallhanging assembly diagram.

FOUR-PATCH BLOCKS

> **Note:** *These blocks are intended to be scrappy. Mix the textures, being mindful of the fabric weights. Try not to place two heavy fabrics next to each other.*

1. Select 4 squares 2″ × 2″ from the assorted mixed-medium fabrics. Vary the colors and textures.

2. Sew 2 sets of 2 squares each. Press toward the lighter-weight fabric.

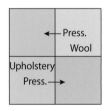

3. Nest the seams with right sides together and sew the 2 pairs together. The block should measure 3½″ × 3½″ and will finish in the project at 3″ × 3″. Repeat to make 3 Four-Patch blocks.

FLYING GEESE BLOCKS

1. Draw a diagonal line from corner to corner on the wrong side of each brown square.

2. Place 1 square on the left side of each 2″ × 3½″ gold strip, right

sides together. Stitch on the drawn diagonal line. Trim the seam to ¼″, and press the remaining triangle away from the gold center.

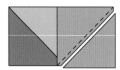

3. Add a second brown square to the right side of the completed unit. Stitch on the drawn diagonal line, trim, and press as shown.

The block should measure 2″ × 3½″ and will finish in the project at 1½″ × 3″. Make 14 Flying Geese blocks.

PINWHEEL BLOCKS

Refer to Wool (page 7) for sewing with wool.

TIP • Triangle paper (2″ finished size) can be used to make the half-square triangle units for this block, or you can construct them in the traditional manner that follows.

1. Draw a diagonal line from corner to corner on the wrong side of each 2⅞″ gold square.

2. Pair a green woven wool square with a gold cotton square. Align the raw edges, right sides together, and stitch ¼″ on each side of the drawn diagonal line.

3. Cut on the line and press toward the gold cotton.

4. Trim the units to 2½″ × 2½″.

5. Join 4 half-square triangle units to create a Pinwheel block. Make 3.

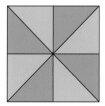

Pinwheel block

TIP • Press the seams open to reduce bulk.

Quilt Assembly

1. Sew the strips and Four-Patch blocks into 5 columns following the fabric placement diagram (page 28).

2. Working from left to right, sew the columns together along their long edges. Press the seams toward the right. Set this section aside.

3. Lay out the remaining pieced section of the background on a flat surface.

4. Sew 2 squares 2½" × 2½" together. Press. Sew the unit to one side of a Pinwheel block. Press the seam toward the squares and away from the Pinwheel block. Repeat for each Pinwheel block.

5. Join the remaining squares into 3 rows of 3 squares each.

6. Lay out and stitch the units together as shown.

7. Sew this section to the right side of the section assembled in Step 2. This center background will measure 18½" × 21½".

8. Sew together 2 rows of 7 Flying Geese blocks along their short sides. With the points in both rows facing in the same direction, press the seams in one row to the right and the other row to the left. The rows will measure 2" × 21½".

9. Add the Flying Geese row that was pressed to the right to the top and the Flying Geese row that was pressed to the left to the bottom of the assembled background, with the gold geese all pointing toward the center. Match the seams with the columns of the background. Press the seams toward the background.

10. Add the side borders.

11. Add the top and bottom borders. The wallhanging will measure 25½" × 25½".

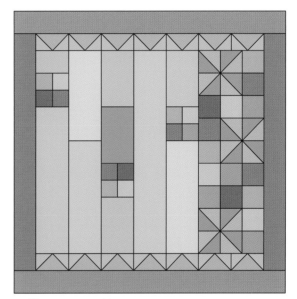

Wallhanging assembly

Appliqué

Refer to Techniques and Wool Appliqué … My Way (page 12).

1. Prepare the appliqué pieces using the project patterns (below, next page, and pages 34 and 35).

2. Referring to the project photo, lay out all the appliqué elements.

3. Couch the yarn stems in place (see Couching, page 18). Secure the ends of both yarns together in the area beneath the flower head with a pin. Twist the 2 yarns together to achieve the desired thickness and texture. Pin loosely in place and couch with wool thread to match the yarn.

TIP • I began each stem with two lengths of green yarn (one thick and one textural) approximately 1½ times the length needed to reach from behind the flower head to the base.

4. Trim the yarn at the base of the stem, making sure the yarn will be concealed under the appliquéd leaves.

5. Appliqué the leaves, pods, and flower elements in place. Work from the background up, as indicated by the dotted lines and the letter codes on the patterns.

6. Embellish the flower pods with bullion knots (page 18) using perle cotton #8.

TIP • Add any beaded embellishments *after* the project is quilted.

Finishing

1. Layer, baste, and quilt as desired.

2. Add binding (page 16).

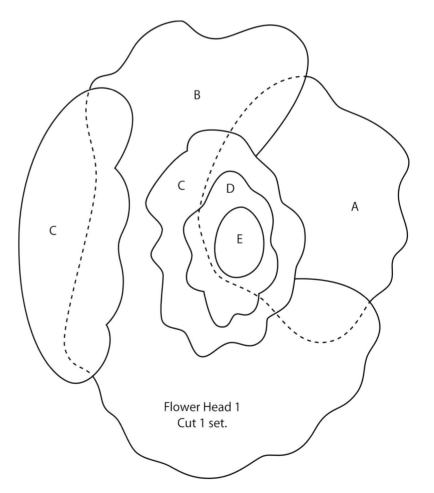

Flower Head 1
Cut 1 set.

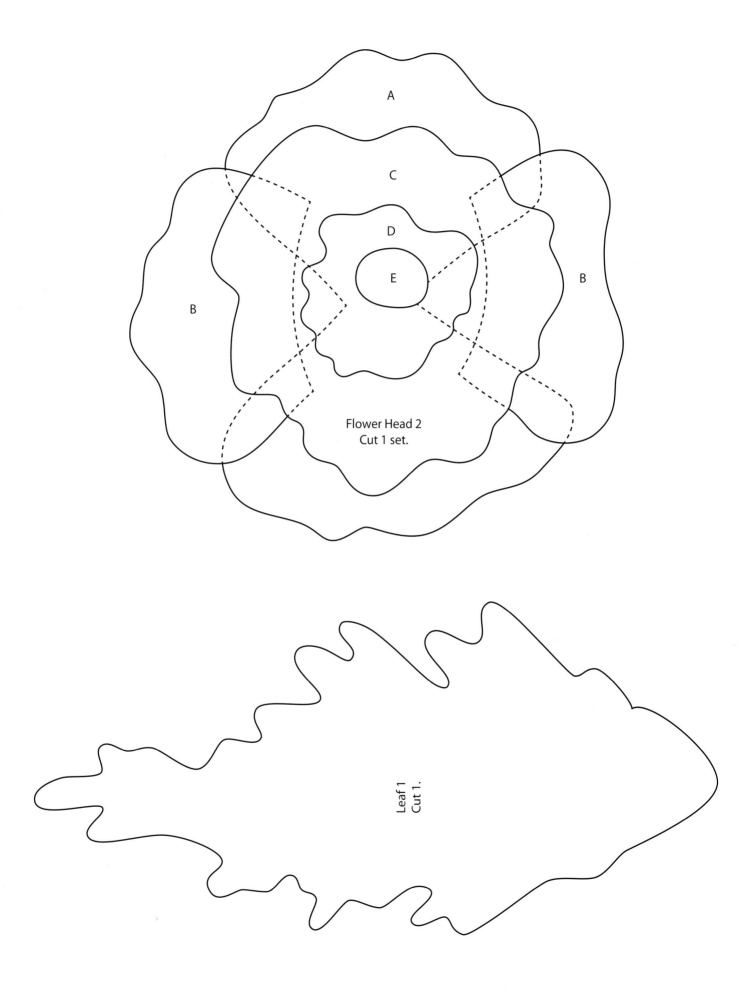

A

C

D

E

B

B

Flower Head 2
Cut 1 set.

Leaf 1
Cut 1.

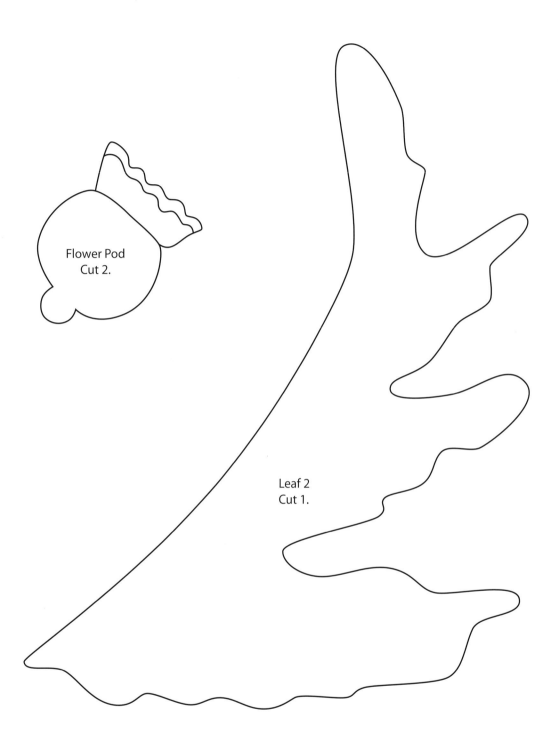

Flower Pod
Cut 2.

Leaf 2
Cut 1.

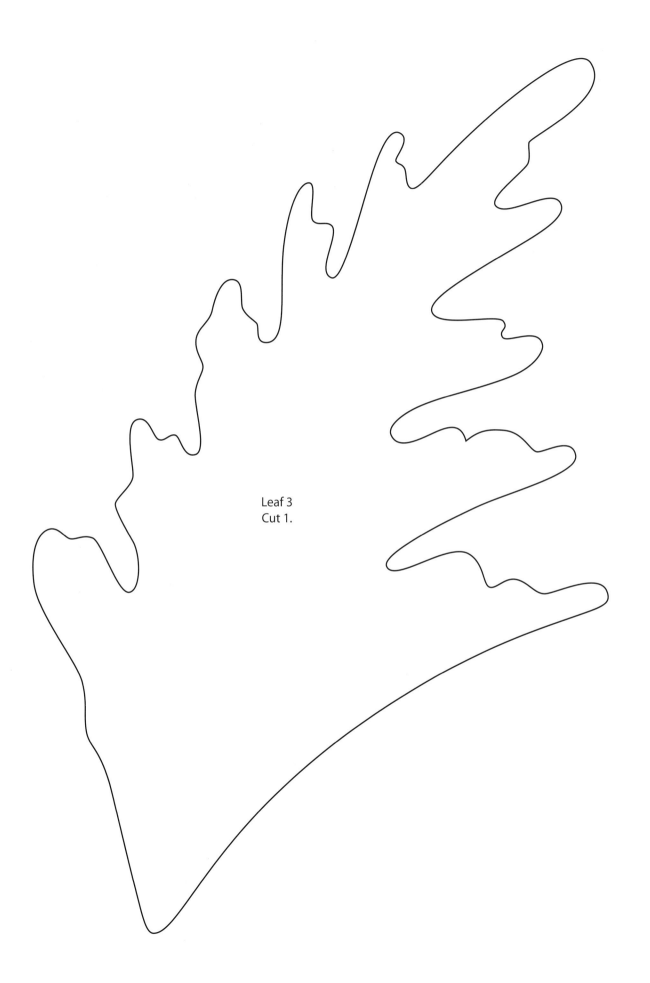

Leaf 3
Cut 1.

Umbrian Fields Throw

Finished blocks: Four-Patch: 3″ × 3″ • Pinwheel: 4″ × 4″ • Square-in-a-Square: 3″ × 3″
Finished throw: 54″ × 75″

The development of the eclectics concept has often been about experimentation and seeking the limits of these new textiles. It has meant experimenting with textiles and their weights when sewn, evaluating the scale of pattern and appliqué, considering texture as a design component, and, of course, always thinking about color. The *Umbrian Fields Throw* is a perfect example of all that. In this project, I was focused on what would happen if large cuts of home decor fabric were used in the body and borders of an otherwise pieced quilt and whether the large-scale wool appliqué would be proportional enough to carry the quilt's interest. The depth of texture on this piece is amazing, and the weight of the home decor textile is actually a comforting plus on a cool evening. None of it presented a problem to my longarm quilter.

Read Exploring New Textiles: Eclectic Fabric Guidelines (page 6) before beginning.

Materials

Fabric requirements are based on a fabric width of at least 40″, except where noted.

FABRICS FOR BORDERS AND BACKGROUND

Gold textured upholstery (at least 56″ wide): 1⅛ yards for quilt body

Brown chenille home decor fabric (at least 56″ wide): ½ yard for borders

Olive-green print: ⅛ yard for inner borders

Cream raw silk: ¼ yard for appliqué background

Gold silk matka: ¼ yard for appliqué background

Gold batik: ¼ yard for appliqué background

Cream/red feather print: ¼ yard for appliqué background

Cream/green shirting print: ¼ yard for appliqué background

Green woven wool: ¼ yard for appliqué background and Pinwheel blocks

FABRICS FOR BLOCKS

Mixed-medium fabrics: 1 yard *total* of at least 7 fabrics for Four-Patch blocks and background squares

Gold cotton print 1: ⅛ yard for Pinwheel blocks

Gold cotton prints 2, 3, and 4: ¼ yard *each* for Square-in-a-Square blocks

Gold brocade home decor upholstery: ¼ yard for Square-in-a-Square blocks

Brown tone-on-tone cotton print: ½ yard for Square-in-a-Square blocks

HAND-DYED WOOL FOR APPLIQUÉ

Reds: Approximately ¼ yard *total* of 3 fabrics for poppies

Greens: Approximately ¼ yard *each* of 3 fabrics (medium and dark) for leaves and pods

Gold *and* black: 4″ × 5″ *each* for poppy details

OTHER MATERIALS

Interfacing for hand-dyed wools and silk

Green yarn: Approximately 9 yards *each* of 2 different textures for stems

Color-coordinating wool thread for appliqué and couching

Perle cotton #8: Valdani #O521 for details on poppy pods (*optional*)

Backing: 5 yards

Binding: ⅝ yard

Batting: 62″ × 83″

Cutting

GOLD TEXTURED UPHOLSTERY

• Cut 1 piece 35½″ × 54½″.

BROWN CHENILLE HOME DECOR FABRIC

• Cut 2 strips 6½″ × 54½″.

OLIVE-GREEN PRINT

• Cut 3 strips 1″ × width of fabric.

CREAM RAW SILK

• Cut 1 strip 3½″ × 18½″ (W).

• Cut 1 strip 3½″ × 10½″ (G).

• Cut 1 strip 3½″ × 8½″ (L).

• Cut 1 strip 3½″ × 5½″ (B).

GOLD SILK MATKA

• Cut 3 strips 3½″ × 6½″ (N).

• Cut 1 strip 3½″ × 5½″ (F).

• Cut 1 strip 3½″ × 4½″ (D).

• Cut 1 square 3½″ × 3½″ (R).

• Cut 2 strips 3½″ × 2½″ (J).

GOLD BATIK

• Cut 1 strip 3½″ × 11″ (Q).

• Cut 1 strip 3½″ × 10½″ (A).

• Cut 1 strip 3½″ × 9½″ (Y).

• Cut 1 strip 3½″ × 8½″ (H).

• Cut 1 strip 3½″ × 8″ (T).

• Cut 2 squares 3½″ × 3½″ (M).

CREAM/RED FEATHER PRINT

• Cut 1 strip 3½″ × 18½″ (C).

• Cut 1 strip 3½″ × 12½″ (S).

• Cut 1 strip 3½″ × 10½″ (K).

• Cut 1 strip 3½″ × 6½″ (X).

• Cut 2 squares 3½″ × 3½″ (O).

CREAM/GREEN SHIRTING PRINT

• Cut 1 strip 3½″ × 13½″ (I).

• Cut 1 strip 3½″ × 11″ (U).

• Cut 1 strip 3½″ × 8″ (P).

GREEN WOVEN WOOL

• Cut 1 strip 3½″ × 7½″ (V).

• Cut 1 strip 3½″ × 6½″ (E).

• Cut 12 squares 2⅞″ × 2⅞″ for the Pinwheel blocks.

MIXED-MEDIUM FABRICS

• Cut 30 squares 2½″ × 2½″ for the background.

• Cut 40 squares 2″ × 2″ for the Four-Patch blocks.

GOLD COTTON PRINT 1

• Cut 12 squares 2⅞″ × 2⅞″ for the Pinwheel blocks.

GOLD COTTON PRINTS 2, 3, AND 4

• Cut 14 squares 2½″ × 2½″ from *each* of the 3 golds.

GOLD BROCADE HOME DECOR UPHOLSTERY

• Cut 14 squares 2½″ × 2½″.

BROWN TONE-ON-TONE COTTON PRINT

• Cut 108 squares 2½″ × 2½″; cut each square diagonally once.

BINDING

• Cut 7 strips 2½″ × width of fabric.

Note: Cut all the fabrics before you begin to assemble the top. Any leftovers can be added into the mix for the appliqué background area. Adding small elements from the other areas of the quilt into the appliqué background will give the project continuity.

The background for the appliqué is intended to have a random, scrappy kind of feel. Do not worry that your appliqué shapes may partially cover some of the sparks of color contributed by the Four-Patch blocks. Positioning a leaf or flower head partially over a block is perfectly fine—in fact, probably better. Allow the block to peek out from behind the images, layering the interest of the textures and colors.

Construction

All seam allowances are ¼″ unless otherwise noted. Construct all the block elements of the project before joining the columns shown in the appliqué background assembly diagram.

FOUR-PATCH BLOCKS

Note: These blocks are intended to be scrappy. Mix the textures, being mindful of the fabric weights. Try not to place two heavy fabrics next to each other.

1. Select 4 squares 2″ × 2″ from the assorted mixed-medium fabrics. Vary the colors and textures.

2. Sew 2 sets of 2 squares each. Press toward the lighter-weight fabric.

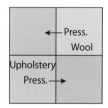

3. Nest the seams with right sides together and sew the 2 pairs together. The block should measure 3½″ × 3½″ and will finish in the project at 3″ × 3″. Repeat to make 10 Four-Patch blocks.

PINWHEEL BLOCKS

Refer to Wool (page 7) for sewing with wool.

TIP • Triangle paper (2″ finished size) can be used to make the half-square triangle units for this block, or you can construct them in the traditional manner that follows.

1. Draw a diagonal line from corner to corner on the wrong side of each 2⅞″ gold print 1 square.

2. Pair a green woven wool square with a gold print 1 square. Align the raw edges, right sides together, and stitch ¼″ on each side of the drawn diagonal line.

3. Cut on the line and press toward the gold print.

4. Trim the units to 2½″ × 2½″.

5. Join 4 half-square triangle units, as shown. The blocks will measure 4½″ × 4½″ and will finish 4″ × 4″. Make 6 Pinwheel blocks.

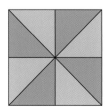

SQUARE-IN-A-SQUARE BLOCKS

Note: You will have a couple extras of the 2½″ gold squares used as the centers of the Square-in-a-Square blocks, but the additional quantity will give you variety to play with.

1. Find the centerlines of 54 assorted gold 2½″ squares, and finger-press a crease both horizontally and vertically on each square.

2. Center a brown triangle on a crease line; align the raw edges, right sides together, and sew a ¼″ seam. Repeat the process to sew a brown triangle to the opposite side. Repeat for each of the 54 center squares.

3. Press away from the center.

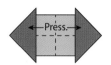

4. Add 2 brown triangles to the 2 remaining sides of each of the 54 gold squares. Align the centers in the same manner.

5. Press away from the center.

6. Trim the blocks to 3½″ × 3½″ using the 45° angle on your ruler, or use one of the many rulers available for trimming this unit accurately. Take care to allow for the needed ¼″ seam allowance around the entire block. The blocks will finish in the project at 3″ × 3″. Make 54 Square-in-a-Square blocks.

Quilt Assembly

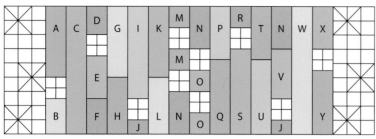

Appliqué background assembly

1. Sew the strips and Four-Patch blocks into 14 columns.

2. Working from left to right, sew the columns together along their long edges. Press the seams toward the right. Set this section aside.

3. Lay out the remaining right- and left-hand sections of the background on a flat surface.

4. Sew 2 squares 2½″ × 2½″ together. Press. Sew them to one side of a Pinwheel block. Repeat for each Pinwheel block.

5. Join the remaining squares into 6 rows of 3 squares each.

6. Lay out and stitch the units together as shown.

7. Sew one section to the left side of the section assembled in Step 2 and the other to the right side. The appliqué background will measure 18½″ × 54½″.

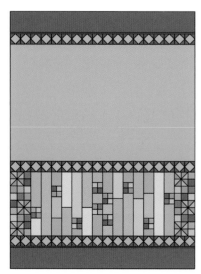

Throw assembly

TIP • Due to the size of this project and the weight of the textiles, it is easier to appliqué this background area now before it is sewn into the body of the quilt. Refer to the instructions in *Umbrian Fields Throw*, Appliqué (next page). You may notice from the photographs that one of the leaves is positioned to overlap onto the bottom Square-in-a-Square block row. If you wish to overlap the leaf, finish all the other appliqué, but wait until your project is assembled to appliqué this element.

8. Join 18 Square-in-a-Square blocks into a row. Press the seams to the left. Make 3 rows, which will each measure 3½″ × 54½″.

9. Add a Square-in-a-Square row to the top of the appliquéd background and another to the bottom. Nest and match the seams with the columns of the background. Press the seams toward the background.

10. Join the 3 olive-green strips end to end. Cut 2 strips 1″ × 54½″. Sew 1 strip to each of the 2 brown chenille border strips. Press toward the olive strips.

11. Add the remaining row of Square-in-a-Square blocks to the top border strip. Press toward the olive strip.

12. Add the top section to the top of the gold textured-upholstery piece. Press the seam open.

13. Add the appliqué background to the bottom of the quilt body. Press the seam open.

14. Add the bottom border and press toward the olive strip. The quilt top will measure 54½″ × 75½″.

Appliqué

Refer to Techniques and Wool Appliqué … My Way (page 12).

1. Prepare the appliqué pieces following the list at the end of this project.

2. Referring to the project photo, lay out all the appliqué elements.

3. Couch the yarn stems in place (see Couching, page 18). Secure the ends of both yarns together in the area beneath the flower head with a pin. Twist the 2 yarns together to achieve the desired thickness and texture. Pin loosely in place and couch with wool thread to match the yarn.

TIP • I began each stem with two lengths of green yarn (one thick and one textural) approximately 1½ times the length needed to reach from behind the flower head to the base.

4. Trim the yarn at the base of the stem, making sure the yarn will be concealed under the appliquéd leaves.

5. Appliqué the leaves, pods, and flower elements in place. Work from the background up, as indicated by the dotted lines and the letter codes on the patterns.

6. Embellish the flower pods with bullion knots (page 18) using perle cotton #8.

Finishing

1. Layer, baste, and quilt as desired.

2. Add binding (page 16).

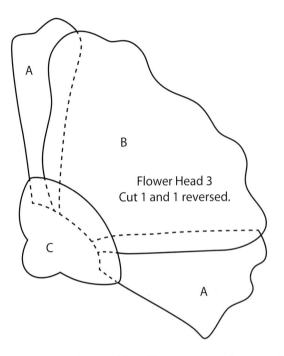

Using the *Umbrian Fields Wallhanging* patterns (pages 32–35), cut the following pieces:

Leaf 1: Cut 2 (1 and 1 reversed).

Leaf 2: Cut 2 (1 and 1 reversed).

Leaf 3: Cut 4 (2 and 2 reversed).

Flower Head 1: Cut 2 (1 and 1 reversed).

Flower Head 2: Cut 2.

Flower Pod: Cut 3.

Umbrian Fields Needlecase

Finished needlecase: 4½″ × 9″ closed, 9″ × 9″ open

What better way to test the flexibility of mixed-medium textiles than to try them in different combinations, in different textures and colorways, and in different project sizes? "How low (small) can you go?" is a catchphrase that occurs to me here in this *Umbrian Fields Needlecase* project. *Very* small would be the answer! With a little textile knowledge in hand, pull together assorted scraps of many fabric types: cotton, batik, linen, silk, upholstery, and more. Add three cotton fat quarters and a few wools, and the possibilities abound.

Read Exploring New Textiles: Eclectic Fabric Guidelines (page 6) before beginning.

Materials

FABRICS FOR EXTERIOR

Assorted mixed-medium scraps, ranging in size from 2″ to 10″ (See Cutting, at right.)

FABRICS FOR INTERIOR

Coordinating cottons: 3 fat quarters (18″ × 20″ *each*)

Woven wool: 8″ × 8½″ for needle keep

HAND-DYED WOOL FOR APPLIQUÉ

Reds: 2 fabrics, *each* 4″ × 4″, for poppy

Greens: 2 fabrics, *each* 4″ × 6″, for leaves

Black: 1½″ × 1½″ for poppy detail

OTHER MATERIALS

Interfacing for hand-dyed wools and silk

Fusible fleece: 10″ × 15″

Green yarn: 18″ *each* of 2 different textures for stem

Color-coordinating wool thread for appliqué and couching

Brown grosgrain ribbon (¼″ wide): 2 yards

Small elastic hair tie

Buttons (½″–⅝″): 1 in yellow for poppy center and 2 in red for interior closures

Cutting

ASSORTED MIXED-MEDIUM SCRAPS

- Cut 1 strip 5¼″ × 7½″ (F).
- Cut 1 strip 2½″ × 5¼″ (E).
- Cut 3 strips 1¼″ × 9½″ (B, C, and D).
- Cut 18 squares 1½″ × 1½″ (A).

COORDINATING COTTONS

- From fat quarter 1, cut 1 strip 5″ × 9½″ for the left background.
- From fat quarter 2, cut 1 strip 5″ × 9½″ for the right background *and* 1 strip 8½″ × 9½″ for the left pocket.
- From fat quarter 3, cut 2 strips 2½″ × 9″ for the left pocket flap *and* 1 strip 5″ × 10½″ for the scissor pocket.

WOVEN WOOL

- Cut 1 strip 7½″ × 8″.

TIP • Cut the woven wool strip with a pinking blade or pinking scissors.

FUSIBLE FLEECE

- Cut 1 square 9¼″ × 9¼″ for the body of the case.
- Cut 1 strip 2½″ × 9″ for the interior pocket flap.

BROWN GROSGRAIN RIBBON

- Cut 1 length 12″ for the scissor ties.
- Cut 2 lengths 10″ *each* for the case ties.

Construction

EXTERIOR

1. Referring to the needlecase exterior layout diagram, arrange the 18 A squares in 2 rows of 9 squares each. Sew the squares together into 2 rows. Press all the seams in one row to the right and the seams in the other row to the left. Each row will measure 1¼″ × 9½″.

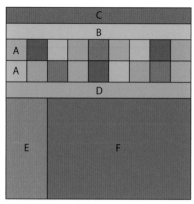

Needlecase exterior layout

Note: Follow the pressing instructions in Exploring New Textiles: Eclectic Fabric Guidelines (page 6). Create opposing seams whenever possible, or press the seams open.

2. Sew the 2 rows together along their long edges, nesting the seams as you go. Press the seam open. The section will measure 2½″ × 9½″.

3. Sew 1 B strip 1¼″ × 9½″ to the top of the pieced squares and 1 D strip 1¼″ × 9½″ to the bottom. Press away from the center.

4. Add the remaining 1¼″ × 9½″ C strip to the top of the B strip. Press toward the C strip.

5. Sew the 2½″ × 5¼″ E strip to the 5¼″ × 7½″ F strip. Press the seam open.

6. Add the unit from Step 5 to the bottom of the horizontal band completed in Step 4. Press toward the D strip.

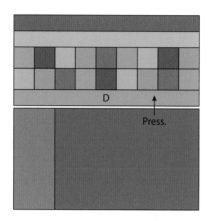

Press.

7. The exterior of the needlecase is now complete and will measure 9½″ × 9½″. Refer to Wool Appliqué … My Way (page 12) to add appliqué to the right-hand side of the pieced background.

8. Once the background is appliquéd, center and fuse the 9¼″ × 9¼″ fleece to the wrong side of the needlecase exterior.

Note: The fusible fleece is cut smaller than the needlecase to reduce bulk in the final seam allowance. You may quilt as desired, but quilting is optional.

INTERIOR

1. Fold the left pocket in half, wrong sides together. It will measure 4¼″ × 9½″. Press.

2. Referring to the interior assembly diagram, place the folded pocket on top of the left background piece. Align the raw edges on 3 sides.

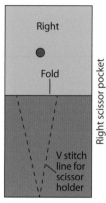

Interior assembly

3. Fold the scissor pocket in half, wrong sides together. It will measure 5″ × 5¼″.

4. Place the folded pocket on the right-hand background section. Align the raw edges on 3 sides.

5. Stitch a V in the right-hand scissor pocket. Begin stitching ½″ from the left edge of the pocket. This section will hold the scissors in place. You can center the V or place it a little to the left of the pocket center.

6. Place the right and left interior pieces together, right sides together, and sew the centerline with a ¼″ seam. Press the seam open.

7. Fuse the 2½″ × 9″ fusible fleece strip to the back of one of the left pocket-flap strips.

8. Center the hair tie on this section, extending it approximately ½″ beyond the edge.

9. Layer the 2 pocket-flap strips right sides together, and sew along 3 sides (1 long side and 2 short sides), catching the hair tie in the seam. Stitch the seam over the hair tie again to secure it.

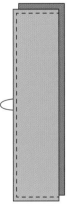

Pocket flap

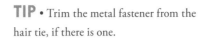

TIP • Trim the metal fastener from the hair tie, if there is one.

10. Trim the corners and turn the flap right side out.

11. Press and topstitch ¼″ in from the finished edges.

12. Layer the pocket flap on the left-hand pocket, centering it as shown in the needlecase interior assembly diagram (at right). Pin and baste in place along the outside raw edge.

13. Fold the 12″ ribbon length in half. Approximately 2″ above the folded edge of the scissor pocket, center the folded ribbon edge over the V-shaped scissor area and tack

it in place. Sew a button on top of the folded edge.

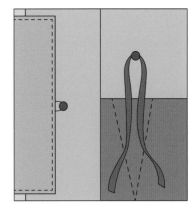

Needlecase interior assembly

TIP • Use this ribbon length to tie your scissors into the case. No more lost scissors!

Assembly

1. Lay the completed needlecase exterior faceup on your work surface. Mark the horizontal center of the case on both vertical edges.

2. Align the edges of the 10″ ribbon lengths with these markings. Extend the ribbon approximately ½″ beyond the edge of the cover. Pin in place.

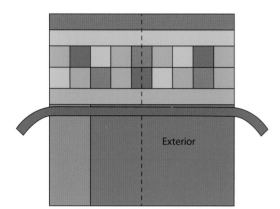

Add ribbon ties.

TIP • The loose ends of the ribbon will remain on the face of the needlecase exterior. Secure them with pins to ensure that they don't get caught in any of the seams around the outside edge of the cover. Depending on the ribbon you have chosen, you may want to dab a little Fray Check on the ends of the ties to keep them from fraying during use.

3. Layer the exterior and interior, right sides together. Align all the raw edges and pin.

4. Stitch through all the layers around the perimeter, leaving an opening at the bottom for turning.

5. Clip the corners and turn the needlecase right side out through the bottom opening. Press and hand stitch the opening closed.

6. Center the woven wool strip on the interior of the needlecase.

7. Stitch along the center seam through all the thicknesses.

8. On the face of the interior left-hand pocket, position a button beneath the hair-tie loop. Stitch in place, catching only the pocket—*not* the background.

9. Sew the yellow button to the center of the flower appliqué on the exterior, being careful not to catch the interior pocket with your stitches.

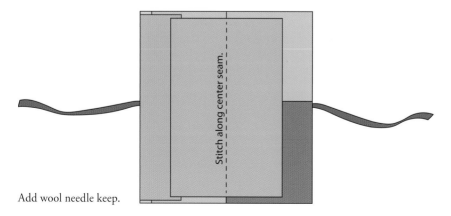

Add wool needle keep.

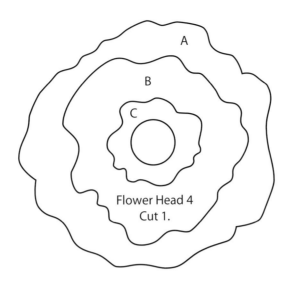

Flower Head 4
Cut 1.

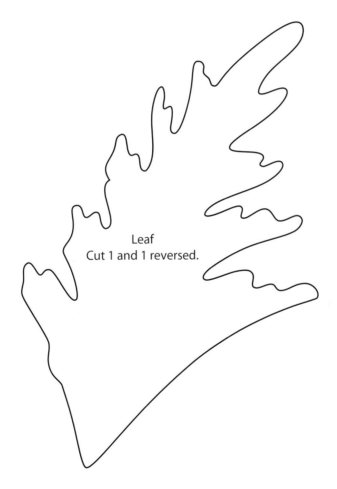

Leaf
Cut 1 and 1 reversed.

Market Tote

THE ART OF MIXING TEXTILES IN QUILTS

Market Tote with Appliqué

Finished blocks: Four-Patch: 3″ × 3″ • Pinwheel: 3″ × 3″
Finished tote: 18″ wide × 16″ high × 8″ deep

The Market Tote project was first conceived to showcase how to use an Eclectic Bundle. Eclectic Bundles, which I still offer today, were the way I first chose to merchandise this mixed-medium textile concept. An Eclectic Bundle is a mix of sixteen different textiles in small cuts that express a colorway and that are diverse in their scale, fiber content, sheen, and texture. A typical bundle could include wools, hand-dyed wools, home decor fabrics, linens, wovens, silks of different types, batiks, and a diverse selection of cottons. Prints could include contemporary designs, reproduction prints, and large- and small-scale motifs. The same result can be achieved with an eclectic scrappy mix drawn from your stash.

This tote pattern offers two variations. They are identical in their shape, form, and basic construction, but there are design differences in how the elements of the bag are articulated. The first version, *Market Tote with Appliqué*, has pieced front and back panels. The front is accented with wool appliqué and couched yarn in one of my favorite motifs: the poppies of the Umbrian region of Italy. The interior size and construction of both bags is the same.

Read Exploring New Textiles: Eclectic Fabric Guidelines (page 6) before beginning.

> *Note: The fabrics selected for the pieced sections of the front and back panels include silk dupioni, silk matka, wool, upholstery-grade brocade, raw silk, linen, batik, and a mix of traditional cottons. Reproduction prints play very nicely with contemporary prints and batiks!*

Materials

FABRICS FOR TOTE CONSTRUCTION

Mixed-medium fabrics: 1 yard *total* of 16 fabrics *or* an Eclectic Bundle for pieced front and back panels

Assorted lights (combination of traditional cottons and silks): ⅜ yard *total* for pieced front and back panels

Tapestry-style home decor upholstery: ⅝ yard for exterior body and sides

Chenille-texture home decor upholstery: ¼ yard for header

Accent cotton: ½ yard for header detail and trim accent

Cotton lining: 1 yard for bag interior

Muslin: ¼ yard for interior bag construction

Fusible fleece: ½ yard for construction

Fusible interfacing: ½ yard for construction (Use 809 Décor-Bond by Pellon or an equivalent. Décor-Bond is 44″ wide; if you use a narrower product, you will need 1 yard.)

HAND-DYED WOOL FOR APPLIQUÉ

Reds: 3 fabrics, *each* approximately 6″ × 8″, for poppies

Greens: 2 fabrics (medium and dark), *each* approximately 13″ × 15″, for leaves and buds

Gold: 3″ × 3″ for poppy details and buds

Black: 3″ × 3″ for poppy centers

OTHER MATERIALS

Interfacing for hand-dyed wools and silk

Green yarn: Approximately 3 yards for couched stems

Color-coordinating wool thread for appliqué and couching

Perle cotton #8 or #5: Gold for French knots

Corrugated plastic: 6″ × 18″ for hidden interior support

Leather handles: 27″–29″ long

Buttonhole thread to match handles (This thread is heavier than regular sewing thread.)

Magnetic clasp (*optional*)

Cutting

To ensure the best results, make sure that all the fabrics are first pressed well and free from folds or wrinkles. Prepare the fabrics as needed by referring to Exploring New Textiles: Eclectic Fabric Guidelines (page 6).

Note: *Use a scrappy mix of the sixteen mixed-medium fabrics and assorted lights to assemble the components of the front and back panels. Letter codes refer to the front and back panel assembly diagrams.*

MIXED-MEDIUM FABRICS

- Cut 10 wool squares 2⅜″ × 2⅜″ for the Pinwheel blocks (B).

- Cut 10 cotton squares 2⅜″ × 2⅜″ for the Pinwheel blocks (C).

- Cut 18 squares 2″ × 2″ for the front panel Four-Patch blocks and squares (A).

- Cut 28 squares 2″ × 2″ for the back panel Four-Patch blocks (A).

ASSORTED LIGHTS— FRONT PANEL

- Cut 1 strip 3½″ × 8″ (K).

- Cut 1 strip 3½″ × 7½″ (J).

- Cut 2 strips 3½″ × 6½″ (H).

- Cut 1 strip 3½″ × 6″ (G).

- Cut 1 strip 3½″ × 5″ (F).

- Cut 2 strips 3½″ × 4½″ (E).

- Cut 2 squares 3½″ × 3½″ (D).

ASSORTED LIGHTS— BACK PANEL

- Cut 1 strip 3½″ × 6½″ (H).

- Cut 2 strips 3½″ × 4½″ (E).

- Cut 4 squares 3½″ × 3½″ (D).

- Cut 2 strips 1½″ × 3½″ (L).

TAPESTRY-STYLE HOME DECOR UPHOLSTERY

- Cut 1 strip 8½″ × 18½″ for the bottom.

- Cut 2 strips 8½″ × 16½″ for the sides.

- Cut 4 strips 3½″ × 16½″ for the front and back panels.

CHENILLE-TEXTURE HOME DECOR UPHOLSTERY

• Cut 2 strips 6½″ × 18½″ for the header.

ACCENT COTTON

• Cut 2 strips 3¾″ × 18½″ for the exterior facing.

• Cut 2 strips 2″ × 18½″ for the interior facing.

COTTON LINING

• Cut 2 strips 16½″ × 18½″ for the front and back lining.

• Cut 2 strips 8½″ × 16½″ for the side lining.

• Cut 1 strip 8½″ × 18½″ for the bottom lining.

MUSLIN

• Cut 1 strip 8½″ × 18½″ for the false bottom in the lining.

FUSIBLE FLEECE

• Cut 2 strips 16″ × 18″.

FUSIBLE INTERFACING

• Cut 2 strips 16½″ × 18½″.

Construction

All seam allowances are ¼" unless otherwise noted.

FOUR-PATCH BLOCKS

These blocks are used in both the front and back panels of the tote.

1. Select 4 different mixed-medium fabric 2″ squares for each block. Do not position 2 heavy fabrics next to each other.

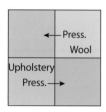

2. Sew the 2 top squares together and press. Sew the 2 bottom squares together and press in the opposite direction.

Note: Press away from the heavier home decor and wool fabrics. Their positions in the block will dictate the direction of the pressing.

3. Join the 2 rows of squares along their long edges. "Twirl" the resulting seam by gently pulling at the outside edges of the resulting block. Press. This will help achieve the flattest possible front.

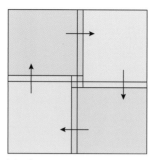

Twirling seams

4. The block should measure 3½″ × 3½″ and will finish in the panels at 3″ × 3″. Make 11 Four-Patch blocks. You will have 2 remaining 2″ squares; sew these together.

PINWHEEL BLOCKS

These blocks are used in the back panel of the tote. The pairing of wool with cotton fabrics for these pinwheels makes it easier to create sharp points. Refer to Wool (page 7) for sewing with wool.

1. Draw a diagonal line from corner to corner on the wrong side of each 2⅜″ cotton square.

2. Pair a wool square and a cotton square. Align the raw edges, right sides together, and stitch ¼″ on each side of the drawn diagonal line.

3. Cut on the drawn line and press away from the wool.

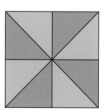

4. Each pairing will yield 2 half-square triangle units. You will have 20 half-square triangle units total; each should measure 2″ × 2″. Trim as required.

5. Sew 4 half-square triangle units together, as shown. Twirl the final seam. Press.

Pinwheel block

6. The block will measure 3½″ × 3½″ and will finish at 3″ × 3″ in the back panel. Make 5 Pinwheel blocks.

FRONT AND BACK PANELS

1. For each panel, assemble 4 columns, inserting the Four-Patch blocks and the Pinwheel blocks as shown. The letter codes refer to the patches in the cutting instructions. Each column will measure 3½″ × 16½″. The top 3″ of each panel will be covered by the header.

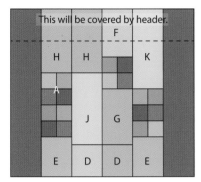

Front panel assembly

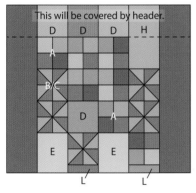

Back panel assembly

2. Sew the 4 columns of each panel together, working from left to right. Press the seams in one direction.

3. Sew a 3½″ × 16½″ tapestry-style home decor strip to each side of each assembled panel. Press the seams away from the panels. The panels will measure 16½″ × 18½″.

Appliqué

Refer to Techniques and Wool Appliqué … My Way (page 12).

1. Prepare all the appliqué pieces using the project patterns (pages 56 and 57).

2. Referring to the project photo, lay out all the appliqué elements.

3. Couch the yarn stems in place (see Couching, page 18). Secure the ends of both yarns together in the area beneath the flower head with a pin. Twist the 2 yarns together to achieve the desired thickness and texture. Pin loosely in place and couch with wool thread to match the yarn.

TIP • I began each stem with two lengths of green yarn (one thick and one textural) approximately 1½ times the length needed to reach from behind the flower head to the base.

4. Trim the yarn at the base, making sure the yarn will be concealed under the appliquéd leaves, or couch it all the way to the bottom of the panel so it can be caught in the seam.

5. Appliqué the leaves, pods, and flower elements in place. Work from the background up, as indicated by the dotted lines and letter codes on the appliqué patterns.

6. Embellish the flower centers with French knots (page 19) using perle cotton #8 or #5.

Finishing

TOTE ASSEMBLY

1. Center a strip of fusible fleece on the wrong side of each pieced panel and fuse according to the manufacturer's instructions.

> **Note:** *The fleece is cut ½″ smaller than the dimensions of the panels so that it will not be caught in the seams. Sewing the fleece into the seams would only create unwanted bulk.*

2. Quilt the front and back panels as desired.

3. Sew an 8½″ × 16½″ tapestry-style home decor strip to each side of the front panel. Sew these seams from top to bottom. End the stitching ¼″ before you reach the bottom edge; back tack.

4. In the same manner, join the back panel to the 2 remaining edges of the side pieces. Stop stitching ¼″ before you reach the bottom of the panel; back tack.

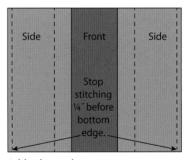

Add side panels.

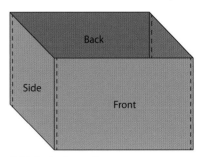

Add the back panel.

5. Finish all the seams with a machine zigzag stitch, stopping ¼″ above the bottom edge. This will make the bag stronger and help reduce fraying on the edges of the home decor fabrics.

6. Press the seams away from the side panels.

7. Sew the 8½″ × 18½″ tapestry-style home decor strip to the base of the three-dimensional rectangle just created: Pin the panel in place, right sides together. Stitch using a ¼″ seam, following the tote bottom construction diagrams. Begin on one of the 8½″ sides. Begin stitching ¼″ down from the top edge, and stop stitching ¼″ before you reach the end (Step 1). Working clockwise around the base, sew the next 2 seams in the same manner, but start the seam at the top edge. Stop sewing ¼″ before reaching the end of the seam (Steps 2 and 3). For the last remaining seam, sew the entire length of the seam end to end.

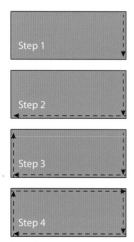

Tote bottom construction

8. Finish all 4 seams with a machine zigzag stitch.

9. Turn the bag right side out, pushing out the corners from the inside and making them square.

SIDE PANEL PLEATS

1. On each side panel, find and mark the centerline, approximately 4″ in from each side.

> *Note: Use whatever type of marking is easiest for you to see. Make the marks within the top 3″ of the bag; the header will conceal this area.*

2. Bring the seam edges of the front and back panels together so they meet at the marked centerline of a side panel. Do *not* fold the face of the front or back panel. Pin the panels in place.

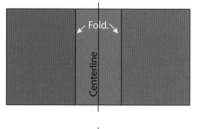

Side panel pleats

3. Stitch a ¼″ seam through all the folded thicknesses along the top edge of the side panel.

4. Parallel to the top edge, mark another line 2¾″ down. Staystitch the folded side panel along this marked line.

5. Repeat Steps 2–4 for the second side panel.

LINING

1. Following the manufacturer's instructions, fuse the interfacing to the wrong side of the 16½″ × 18½″ lining pieces.

2. Fold under ¼″ on a short edge of the 8½″ × 18½″ muslin strip. Topstitch the folded edge.

3. Align 3 edges (2 long and 1 short) of the muslin strip on the wrong side of the 8½″ × 18½″ lining strip. Sew along 3 sides with a scant ¼″ seam. This will be the lining bottom with a pocket for the plastic support piece.

4. Construct the lining in the same manner as described in the construction instructions for the body of the bag. Sew the sides to the front and back panels, and attach the bottom. Make the side panel pleats. Refer to Tote Assembly, Steps 3–8 (page 53 and at left) and Side Panel Pleats, Steps 1–5 (at left).

5. Slide the 6″ × 18″ corrugated plastic strip into the muslin pocket.

6. Place the lining inside the bag with wrong sides together. Match the side seams and align the top edges. Machine baste the top edge of the bag, joining the lining and the body of the bag together.

TIP • If your sewing machine has a free-arm option, use it, as it will make this step easier and less cumbersome.

HEADER

1. Sew together the short ends of 2 chenille-texture home decor 6½″ × 18½″ strips. Press the seam open.

2. Fold the header in half along its length, wrong sides together. Press. This will be the top edge of the bag. Open it up again.

3. In the same manner as you sewed the header, sew together the 2″ × 18½″ accent cotton strips for the interior facing and sew together the 3¾″ × 18½″ accent cotton strips for the exterior facing. All the header pieces will now measure 36½″ long.

4. Sew the 2″ × 36½″ interior facing to one of the long edges of the header. Press the seam toward the header.

5. Sew the 3¾″ × 36½″ exterior facing to the remaining long edge of the header. Press the seam away from the header.

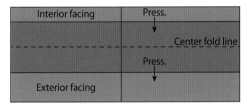

Right side of header strip

6. Sew the 2 short ends of the pieced header strip together, forming a continuous loop. Press the seam open.

7. Fold the interior facing to the inside of the header, wrong sides together, and match the long raw edge. Topstitch close to the folded edge.

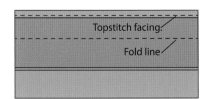

Wrong side of header strip

8. Attach the header to the bag. On the outside of the bag, align the unsewn edge of the exterior facing with the top edge of the bag, right sides together. Match the side seams and ease in any fullness. Securely pin in place.

9. Using the free-arm feature of your sewing machine and a walking foot, sew the header to the top of the bag with a ¼″ seam. Pull the header up and press the seam toward the header. The header will now resemble a collar.

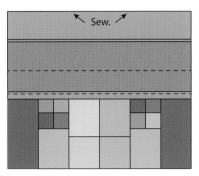

Attach header.

10. Align the pressed edge of the header along the top edge of the bag. Smooth down both sides of the header and securely pin.

Note: The deeper facing on the exterior of the bag will extend ¼″ beyond the edge of the header. It will look like a flange detail. If you wish to add the optional magnetic clasp, center the clasp and attach it following the manufacturer's instructions before topstitching the header in place.

11. Topstitch through all thicknesses on the outside of the bag between the flange and the bottom edge of the header. Topstitch along the top edge.

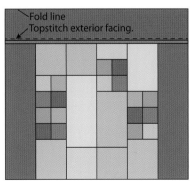

Topstitch.

12. Center the handles on the header and attach.

Note: The handles I used were manufactured by HOBBY & LAND. They had predrilled holes that made the hand stitching easy. Hand stitch the handles in place with a double thickness of buttonhole thread and a sharp chenille needle. I used a back-stitch for added strength.

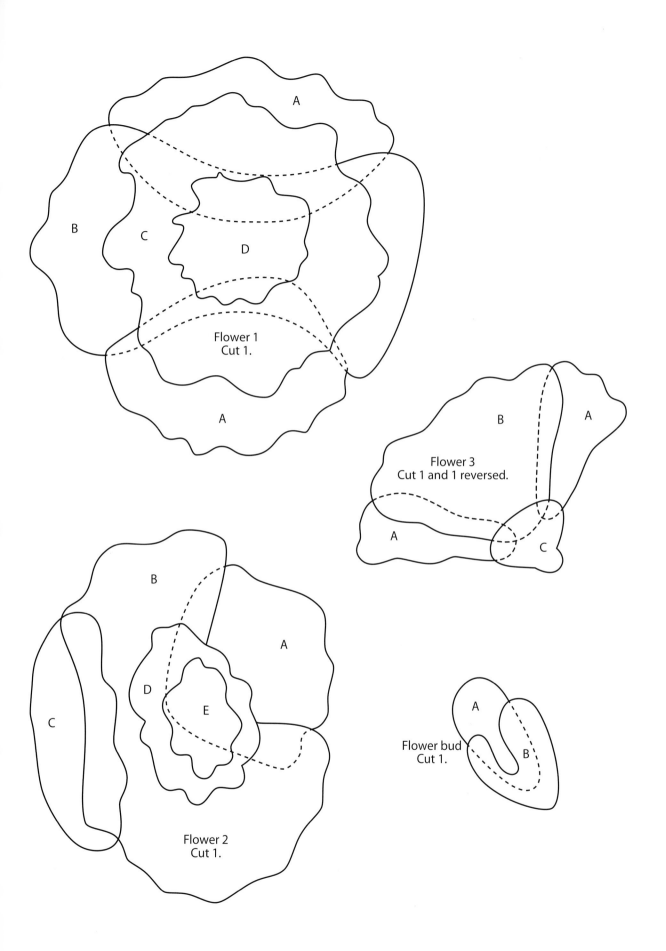

A

B

C

D

Flower 1
Cut 1.

A

B

A

Flower 3
Cut 1 and 1 reversed.

A

C

B

A

C

D

E

Flower 2
Cut 1.

A

Flower bud
Cut 1.

B

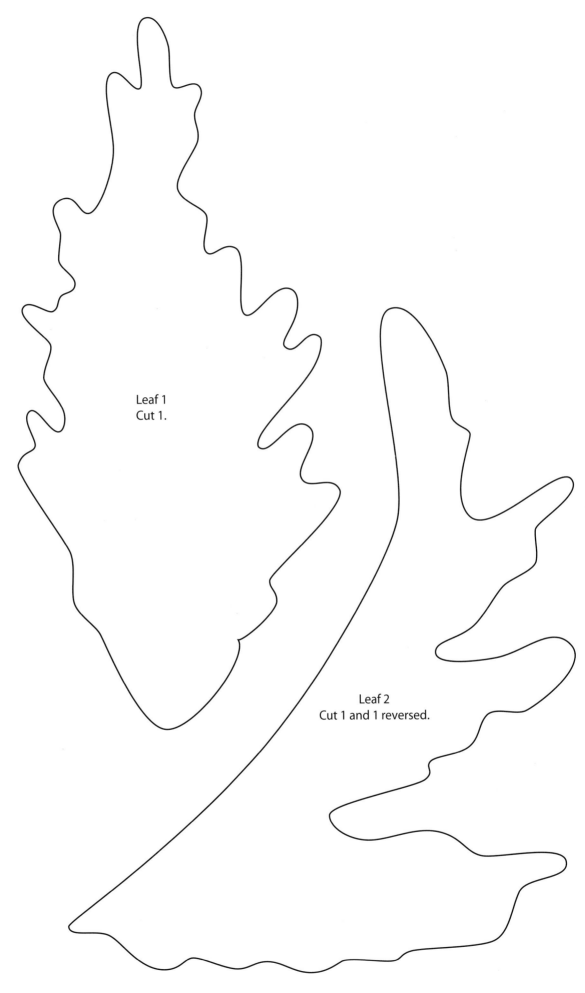

Leaf 1
Cut 1.

Leaf 2
Cut 1 and 1 reversed.

Market Tote with Pieced Header

Finished tote: 18″ wide × 16″ high × 8″ deep

This second version of the Market Tote does not have an appliquéd front but displays its mixed-medium component in a pieced header. Its front and back panels are solid pieces of upholstery fabric, and this version of the tote uses a contrasting fabric at the pleated sides. The construction of the tote is the same as that of the first version. Refer to the diagrams shown in *Market Tote with Appliqué* (page 49).

Read Exploring New Textiles: Eclectic Fabric Guidelines (page 6) before beginning.

Materials

FABRICS FOR TOTE CONSTRUCTION

Mixed-medium fabrics: ½ yard *total* of 16 fabrics *or* 24 assorted scraps, *each* at least 2″ × 7, for pieced header detail

Tapestry-style home decor upholstery (at least 44″ wide): ⅝ yard for front and back panels and bottom

Contrasting home decor upholstery: ⅜ yard for side panels

Accent cotton: ½ yard for header facing

Cotton lining: 1 yard for bag interior

Muslin: ¼ yard for interior bag construction

Fusible fleece: ½ yard for construction

Fusible interfacing: ½ yard for construction (Use 809 Décor-Bond by Pellon or an equivalent. Décor-Bond is 44″ wide; if you use a narrower product, you will need 1 yard.)

OTHER MATERIALS

Interfacing for silks

Corrugated plastic: 6″ × 18″ for hidden interior support

Leather handles: 27″–29″ long

Buttonhole thread to match handles (This thread is heavier than regular sewing thread.)

Magnetic clasp (*optional*)

Cutting

To ensure the best results, make sure that all the fabrics are first pressed well and free from folds or wrinkles. Prepare the fabrics as needed by referring to Exploring New Textiles: Eclectic Fabric Guidelines (page 6).

> **Note:** *Evaluate your fabric selection carefully for the front and back panels before beginning to cut. If you are using a large-scale floral, as shown, you may want to think about the placement of the pattern and how it will be viewed once the tote is assembled. Keep in mind that the header will cover the top 3″ of these panels.*

MIXED-MEDIUM FABRICS

• Cut 24 strips 2″ × 7″.

TAPESTRY-STYLE HOME DECOR UPHOLSTERY

• Cut 2 strips 16½″ × 18½″ for the front and back panels.

• Cut 1 strip 8½″ × 18½″ for the bottom.

CONTRASTING HOME DECOR UPHOLSTERY

• Cut 2 strips 8½″ × 16½″ for the sides.

ACCENT COTTON

• Cut 2 strips 3¾″ × 18½″ for the exterior facing.

• Cut 2 strips 2″ × 18½″ for the interior facing.

COTTON LINING

• Cut 2 strips 16½″ × 18½″ for the front and back lining.

• Cut 2 strips 8½″ × 16½″ for the side lining.

• Cut 1 strip 8½″ × 18½″ for the bottom lining.

MUSLIN

• Cut 1 strip 8½″ × 18½″ for the false bottom in the lining.

FUSIBLE FLEECE

• Cut 2 strips 16″ × 18″.

FUSIBLE INTERFACING

• Cut 2 strips 16½″ × 18½″.

Construction

All seam allowances are ¼″ unless otherwise noted.

Note: The instructions for Market Tote with Appliqué (page 49) include the assembly details for both totes. The sewing instructions for Market Tote with Pieced Header guide you through the differences in the design of the front and back panels and the pieced header construction. Refer to the instructions for Market Tote with Appliqué for tote assembly, construction of the interior lining, and attachment of the header. The front and back panels are single cuts of the tapestry-style home decor upholstery fabric; there is no piecing required.

HEADER

Building the header in two strips rather than a single long strip allows you to visualize the color placement on the front and back panels of the bag. Refer to Exploring New Textiles: Eclectic Fabric Guidelines (page 6) for tips on sewing with specialty fabrics. A walking foot is recommended.

1. Sew together 2 strip sets of 12 strips each, using the 2″ × 7″ mixed-medium strips. Arrange the patterns and textures in a random manner. Press the seams open. The pieced strips will measure 7″ × 18½″.

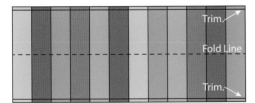

Pieced header

TIP • Take note of where you will be positioning the handles, and try to avoid placing heavy textiles in that section of the header. Depending on the handles you use, the attachment points will likely fall in the third or fourth position in from either end of the strip. Use lighter-weight cottons or cotton blends here, as this will make it much easier to hand sew the handles in place.

2. Trim the strips to 6½″ × 18½″.

Note: Due to their looser weave, wool and home decor fabrics tend to creep or stretch while stitching. Trimming the strip after it is pieced will ensure an even edge.

3. Sew the short ends of the 2 strips together. The resulting strip will measure 6½″ × 36½″.

4. Fold the strip in half lengthwise and press firmly. The crease will mark the finished top edge of the tote.

Assemble the remaining elements of the tote following *Market Tote with Appliqué* (page 49), beginning with Finishing, Tote Assembly.

Bohemian Dance

Life isn't about waiting for the storm to pass.... It's about learning to dance in the rain!

—Vivian Greene

Bohemian Dance Wallhanging

Finished block: 12″ × 12″

Finished wallhanging: 69″ × 69″

Bohemian Dance is about fabric scale, sheen, color play, and secondary patterns. I experimented here with large-scale prints in smaller cuts, disregarding the traditional practice of assigning large prints to border applications. The smaller cuts on the large-scale prints have proven to have more versatility. A small cut will show only a portion of a large print, therefore allowing the same fabric to read differently in various cuts within the same yardage.

There are three types of silk in Bohemian Dance. One of the beauties of silk is the variations of sheen created by different weaves. Color and shine dance throughout, leading your eye around the quilt top. The pattern of diamonds and quarter-squares seemingly on point is an illusion and emerges from the secondary patterning, not the individual block construction.

Bohemian Dance looks complicated but isn't. This is simply a one-block quilt, straight set with a pieced border. The "on-point" diamond patterns and quarter-squares form as the blocks are pieced together. One simple sewing technique is used throughout the construction: connecting corners. Each 12″ finished block is made from four layered 6″ finished squares of the same background. The blocks are all constructed in the same manner; only the backgrounds change.

Read Exploring New Textiles: Eclectic Fabric Guidelines (page 6) before beginning.

> **Note:** *Interface all the silk dupioni before cutting. Also test any other loose weaves to determine whether they would benefit from interfacing before you begin.*

Materials

FABRICS FOR BLOCKS AND BORDERS

Smaller-scale green dot: ⅝ yard
for block A backgrounds

Large-scale brown urns print: 1⅝ yards
for block B backgrounds

Medium-scale blue fountain print: ⅝ yard
for block C backgrounds

Smaller-scale brown/pink print: 1½ yards
for diamond centers and outer border

Teal Radiance silk/cotton blend: 1⅜ yards
for block D backgrounds and inner border

Green Radiance silk/cotton blend: ½ yard
for diamond centers

Turquoise silk dupioni: 1¼ yards for diamond frames

Fuchsia silk matka: 1¼ yards for diamond frames

Rust tonal batik: ½ yard for quarter-squares

Gold silk matka: ½ yard for quarter-squares

HAND-DYED WOOL FOR APPLIQUÉ

Turquoise, cherry, green, gold, *and* fuchsia: Approximately 6″ × 6″ *each* for layered circles and quatrefoil

Greens: Approximately 8½″ × 27″ *each*
of 2 fabrics for leaves

OTHER MATERIALS

Interfacing for hand-dyed wools and silk

Color-coordinated wool thread for appliqué

Backing: 4½ yards

Binding: ⅝ yard

Batting: 77″ × 77″

> *Note: As you work through the pattern, you will likely recognize that there are more efficient ways to build these blocks that would require less fabric, but I really love having what I call the "dividends" left over to build yet another different, but coordinated, project. A twofer, if you will. The Dividends projects (page 98) give you several ideas on how to use these leftovers.*

Cutting

SMALLER-SCALE GREEN DOT

• Cut 16 squares 6½″ × 6½″.

LARGE-SCALE BROWN URNS PRINT

• Cut 48 squares 6½″ × 6½″.

MEDIUM-SCALE BLUE FOUNTAIN PRINT

• Cut 16 squares 6½″ × 6½″.

SMALLER-SCALE BROWN/PINK PRINT

• Cut 120 squares 2″ × 2″.

• Cut 4 squares 5″ × 5″.

• Cut 7 strips 3½″ × width of fabric.

TEAL RADIANCE SILK/COTTON BLEND

• Cut 20 squares 6½″ × 6½″.

• Cut 7 strips 2″ × width of fabric.

GREEN RADIANCE SILK/COTTON BLEND

• Cut 120 squares 2″ × 2″.

TURQUOISE SILK DUPIONI

• Cut 120 squares 3½″ × 3½″.

FUCHSIA SILK MATKA

• Cut 120 squares 3½″ × 3½″.

RUST TONAL BATIK

• Cut 122 squares 2″ × 2″.

GOLD SILK MATKA

• Cut 122 squares 2″ × 2″.

BINDING

• Cut 8 strips 2½″ × width of fabric.

Construction

Sew all the seams with an accurate ¼" seam allowance. Follow the pressing instructions in the diagrams and press consistently throughout the construction process. These instructions will help you achieve opposing seam conditions and make a flatter quilt top. The seams should be pressed on the right side of the blocks. With the silks, take care that your iron is not too hot; do a test sample first. Press from the back if necessary or use a pressing cloth. Consult Exploring New Textiles: Eclectic Fabric Guidelines (page 6).

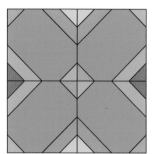
Block A. Make 4.

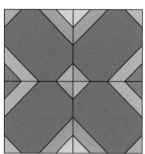
Block B. Make 12.

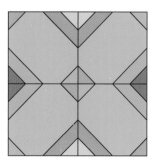
Block C. Make 4.

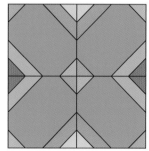
Block D: Appliqué background block. Make 4.

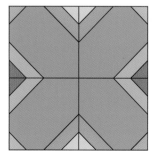
Block E: Center appliqué background block. Make 1.

CONNECTING-CORNERS TECHNIQUE

Draw a diagonal line from corner to corner on the wrong side of a 3½" fuchsia silk matka square. Draw a second line on the square a scant ½" away and parallel to the first drawn line. Layer the marked fuchsia square on a corner of a 6½" background square. Stitch on the drawn lines. Cut between the seams to create a block unit and a dividend unit. Press both units.

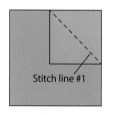
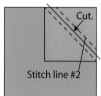
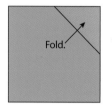

BLOCKS

1. Using the connecting-corners technique, add a 3½" fuchsia square to each 6½" background square for 100 total. Repeat, adding a turquoise silk dupioni square to the opposite corner of each background square.

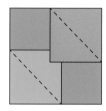

Note: See the Dividend projects (page 98) for ideas on how to use the dividends (leftover half-square triangle units) from this project.

2. Use the connecting-corners technique to add a 2" square on all 4 corners of each background square, following the color placement diagram.

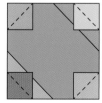
Color placement

Note: Block E, the center block, is constructed in the same manner as the other blocks except that there are no center quarter-squares. The appliqué fills the center of this block instead. In the sample, this means you would make two background squares without a rust tonal batik corner and two without a gold silk matka corner.

3. Press half the pieced squares as shown in pressing diagram 1 and half as shown in pressing diagram 2.

 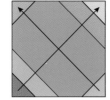

Pressing 1   Pressing 2

Note: It is important to the quilt's secondary pattern that you maintain the correct color orientation of the blocks while sewing. Opposing seams will result in flatter blocks with better pattern joins. Refer to the block diagrams for color orientation.

Note: Refer to the pressing direction of the units before assembly. The arrows indicate the pressing direction of the seams joining the block.

4. Assemble 4 pieced squares with the same background. Choose 2 squares following pressing diagram 1 and 2 following pressing diagram 2. Lay out the squares as they will appear in the quilt top, making sure that the pressing directions alternate and the color placement follows the block diagram.

5. Sew together the 2 top pieced squares. Press to the right.

6. Sew together the 2 bottom pieced squares. Press to the left.

7. Sew the 2 rows together, matching and pinning the opposing seams as needed. Press the center seams of the blocks B down. Press the center seams of all the other blocks up.

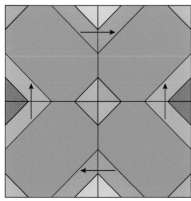

Block

8. The assembled blocks will measure 12½″ × 12½″ and will finish at 12″ × 12″. Make 25 blocks as follows:

    4 blocks A   12 blocks B   4 blocks C

    4 blocks D   1 block E

Appliqué

Refer to Wool Appliqué … My Way (page 12) and appliqué all the pieces before joining the blocks into rows.

1. Prepare all the appliqué pieces using the project patterns (page 67).

2. Lay out all the appliqué pieces on the 4 blocks D and 1 block E.

3. Layer the wool circles. Appliqué the larger circles first and follow with the smaller circles.

Quilt Center Assembly

1. Join the completed 12½″ × 12½″ blocks into 5 rows of 5 blocks each. Follow the placement in the quilt assembly diagram.

2. Press the rows in alternating directions.

3. Sew the rows together. Press the seams in one direction. The quilt top will now measure 60½″ × 60½″.

Border Assembly

The borders for Bohemian Dance are pieced and give the illusion of an inner and outer border that is continuous but pierced by the diamond pattern of the blocks. As a designer, I prefer patterns to finish, and I love the illusion of floating elements.

1. Sew together a 2″ × width of fabric teal silk/cotton-blend strip and a 3½″ × width of fabric brown/pink print strip to make a strip set. Make 7. The strip sets will measure 5″ × width of fabric.

2. Subcut the strip sets into 40 border 5″ × 6½″ strips.

3. Build connecting corners on the lower *right* corners of 10 of the border strips using 3½″ fuchsia squares. Build connecting corners on the lower *left* corners of 10 of the border strips using 3½″ fuchsia squares.

4. Build connecting corners on the lower *right* corners of 10 of the border strips using 3½″ turquoise squares. Build connecting corners on the lower *left* corners of 10 of the border strips using 3½ turquoise squares.

5. Add the 2″ squares in the same manner, following the color orientations shown in the border block F and G diagrams.

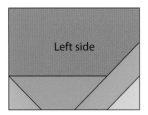
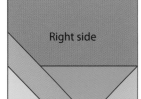

Border block F

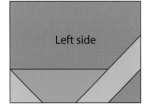

Border block G

6. Pair the matching right and left units. Sew together along the 5″ sides. Make 10 border blocks F and 10 border blocks G, each measuring 5″ × 12½″.

7. To make the corner blocks of the border, add a 2″ gold silk matka square to a corner of a 5″ brown/pink print square. Make 2. Add a 2″ rust tonal batik square to a corner of a 5″ brown/pink print square. Make 2. The corner blocks will measure 5″ × 5″.

8. Sew together 5 border blocks F end to end. The row will measure 5″ × 60½″. Make 2. Press to the right. These are the top and bottom borders.

9. Sew together 5 border blocks G end to end. The row will measure 5″ × 60½″. Make 2. Press to the right. These are the side borders.

10. Sew the top and bottom borders to the quilt top, matching the fuchsia diamonds and the color rhythm of the quarter-squares. Press toward the inner border.

Quilt assembly

11. Add a corner block to each end of both side borders, matching the rhythm of the colors. Press toward the center of the row.

12. Sew the side borders to the quilt top, matching the turquoise diamonds and the color rhythm of the quarter-squares. The quilt top will measure 69″ × 69″.

Finishing

1. Layer, baste, and quilt as desired.

2. Add binding (page 16).

Leaf
Cut 20.

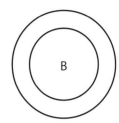

Wool Penny
1⅛″-diameter base with ¾″-diameter circle
Cut 5 sets of 4—20 sets total.

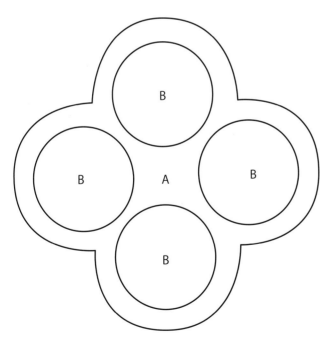

Cut 1.
Cut 4 circles 1⅛″ in diameter.

Wool Penny
¾″-diameter base with ½″-diameter circle
Cut 5 sets of 4—20 sets total.

Bohemian Dance Queen/King Quilt

Finished block: 12″ × 12″ • **Finished quilt:** 94″ × 94″

Bohemian Dance was so named because of its happy Bohemian-looking fabrics that seem to dance across the quilt top. The *Bohemian Dance Queen/King Quilt* has a much more sophisticated appearance than the wallhanging and a smooth elegance that is more like a waltz, hence its original name of *Urban Waltz*. The glorious floral fabric is used in both the background blocks *and* the outer border. The inner border is silk dupioni.

The *Bohemian Dance Queen/King Quilt* can be made even larger by increasing the size of the outer border strips to 8″ × width of fabric instead of 4″ × width of fabric. The finished size, with enlarged border cuts, will be 102″ × 102″.

Read Exploring New Textiles: Eclectic Fabric Guidelines (page 6) before beginning.

Materials

Gray large-scale floral print: 3⅜ yards for block A backgrounds and outer border

Light gray print: 3 yards for block B backgrounds

Taupe Radiance silk/cotton blend: 1¼ yards for block C backgrounds

Red silk dupioni: 1⅝ yards for diamond frames and alternating centers

Gray stripe: 1⅝ yards for diamond frames and alternating centers

Cream textured-silk home decor fabric: 2¼ yards for diamond frames

Gold print: ¾ yard for diamond centers

Dark silk print: ¾ yard for quarter-squares

Brown print: ¾ yard for quarter-squares

Bronze silk dupioni: ¾ yard for inner border

Interfacing for silks

Backing: 8½ yards

Binding: ⅞ yard

Batting: 102″ × 102″

Cutting

GRAY LARGE-SCALE FLORAL PRINT

- Cut 64 squares 6½″ × 6½″.
- Cut 4 squares 5½″ × 5½″.
- Cut 10 strips 4″ × width of fabric.

LIGHT GRAY PRINT

- Cut 96 squares 6½″ × 6½″.

TAUPE RADIANCE SILK/COTTON BLEND

- Cut 36 squares 6½″ × 6½″.

RED SILK DUPIONI

- Cut 112 squares 3½″ × 3½″.
- Cut 112 squares 2″ × 2″.

GRAY STRIPE

- Cut 112 squares 3½″ × 3½″.
- Cut 112 squares 2″ × 2″.

CREAM TEXTURED-SILK HOME DECOR FABRIC

- Cut 224 squares 3½″ × 3½″.

GOLD PRINT

- Cut 224 squares 2″ × 2″.

DARK SILK PRINT

- Cut 226 squares 2″ × 2″.

BROWN PRINT

- Cut 226 squares 2″ × 2″.

BRONZE SILK DUPIONI

- Cut 10 strips 2″ × width of fabric.

BINDING

- Cut 10 strips 2½″ × width of fabric.

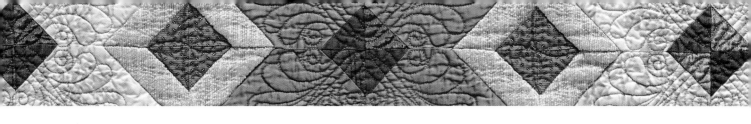

Construction

Follow the instructions for the *Bohemian Dance Wallhanging* for the general construction of this project. Keep in mind that the color orientation of the framed diamonds in the *Bohemian Dance Queen/King Quilt* is slightly different. The strong-colored diamond frames in the *Bohemian Dance Wallhanging* are organized row by row—that is, one row is fuchsia diamond frames, the next row is turquoise, and then it repeats. Assembling one row with red silk dupioni frames and then one row with gray diamond frames in this quilt would result in the red rows being the only rows you would see. The red is too dominant. To balance the color better, I alternated the diamonds in all the rows and let the secondary cream textured-silk diamond frames recede visually. This required careful placement of the color during construction. A design wall where you can arrange the whole project is a great asset.

As with the *Bohemian Dance Wallhanging*, this quilt is a single-block quilt with pieced borders. The "on-point" diamond patterns and quarter-squares form as the blocks are pieced together. One simple technique is used throughout the construction: connecting corners. Each 12″ finished block is made from four layered 6″ finished squares of the same background. To facilitate the color placement of the layered connecting corners, half the blocks, regardless of their background, will be oriented as shown in pressing diagram 1, and the remaining half will be oriented as shown in pressing diagram 2. Follow the diagrams carefully.

CONNECTING-CORNERS TECHNIQUE

Draw a diagonal line from corner to corner on the wrong side of a 3½″ square. Draw a second line on the square a scant ½″ away and parallel to the first drawn line. Layer the marked square on a corner of a 6½″ background square. Stitch on the drawn lines. Cut between the seams to create a block unit and a dividend unit. Press both units open.

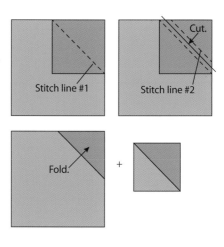

BLOCKS

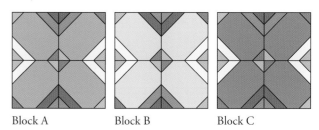

Block A   Block B   Block C

1. Using the connecting-corners technique, add 3½″ red silk dupioni squares to the upper right corners of half the 6½″ block A gray floral print squares. Trim and press.

2. On the remaining 6½″ block A squares, add 3½″ gray stripe squares to the upper right corners. Trim and press.

3. Add 3½″ cream home decor squares to the lower left corners of all the block A squares from Steps 1 and 2.

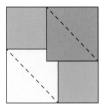

4. Using the connecting-corners technique, add a 2″ square on all 4 corners of each block A square, following the color placement in the block A diagram.

5. Press half the A units as shown in pressing diagram 1 and half as shown in pressing diagram 2.

Pressing 1   Pressing 2

Note: It is important to the quilt's secondary pattern that you place the fabrics in the correct color orientation. Opposing seams will result in flatter blocks with better pattern joins. Refer to the block diagram for color orientation.

6. Repeat Steps 1–5 using the 6½″ block B squares to make 96 B units.

7. Repeat Steps 1–5 using the 6½″ block C squares to make 36 C units.

Note: See the Dividend projects (page 98) for ideas on how to use the dividends (leftover half-square triangle units).

Note: Refer to the pressing direction of the units before assembly. The arrows indicate the pressing direction of the seams joining the block.

8. Arrange 4 units of the same background. Choose 2 squares following pressing diagram 1 and 2 following pressing diagram 2. Lay out the units as they will appear in the quilt top, making sure that the pressing directions alternate and the color placement follows the block diagrams.

9. Sew together the 2 top units. Press to the right.

10. Sew together the 2 bottom units. Press to the left.

11. Sew the 2 rows together, matching and pinning the opposing seams as needed. Press the center seams of blocks A and C up. Press the center seams of blocks B down.

12. The assembled blocks will measure 12½″ × 12½″ and will finish at 12″ × 12″. Make 49 blocks, as follows:

16 blocks A   24 blocks B   9 blocks C

Quilt Center Assembly

1. Join the completed 12½″ × 12½″ blocks into 7 rows of 7 blocks each. Follow the quilt assembly diagram (next page).

2. Press the rows in alternating directions.

3. Sew the rows together. Press the seams in one direction. The quilt top will now measure 84½″ × 84½″.

Border Assembly

The borders for the Bohemian Dance Queen/King Quilt *are constructed in exactly the same manner as the* Bohemian Dance Wallhanging *borders, except for the color distribution and the number of units.*

1. Sew together a 2″ × width of fabric bronze silk dupioni strip and a 4″ × width of fabric gray floral print strip to make a strip set. Make 10. The strip sets will measure 5½″ × width of fabric.

2. Subcut the strip sets into 56 border strips 5½″ × 6½″.

3. Build connecting corners on the lower *right* corners of 7 of the border strips using 3½″ gray squares. Build connecting corners on the lower *left* corners of 7 of the border strips using 3½″ gray squares.

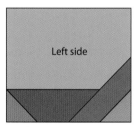

Border block D

4. Build connecting corners on the lower *right* corners of 7 of the border strips using 3½″ red squares. Build connecting corners on the lower *left* corners of 7 of the border strips using 3½″ red squares.

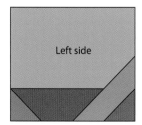
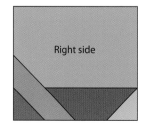

Border block E

5. Build connecting corners on the lower *right* corners of 14 of the border strips using 3½″ cream squares. Build connecting corners on the lower *left* corners of 14 of the border strips using 3½″ cream squares.

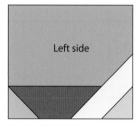
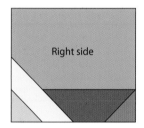

Border block F

6. Add the 2″ squares in the same manner, following the color orientation shown in the border block D, E, and F diagrams.

7. Pair the matching right and left units. Sew together along the 5½″ sides. Make 7 border blocks D, 7 border blocks E, and 14 border blocks F, each measuring 5½″ × 12½″.

8. To make the corner blocks of the border, add a 2″ dark silk print square to a corner of a 5½″ gray floral print square. Make 2. Add a 2″ brown print square to a corner of a 5½″ gray floral print square. Make 2. The corner blocks will measure 5½″ × 5½″.

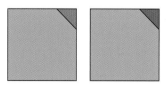

9. Sew together 4 border blocks E and 3 border blocks D end to end, alternating the colors of the framed diamonds. The row will measure 5½" × 84½". Press to the right. This is the top border.

10. Sew together 4 border blocks D and 3 border blocks E end to end, alternating the colors of the framed diamonds. The row will measure 5½" × 84½". Press to the right. This is the bottom border.

11. Sew together 7 border blocks F end to end. The row will measure 5½" × 84½". Make 2. Press to the right. These are the side borders.

12. Sew the top and bottom borders to the quilt top, matching the red and gray diamonds and the color rhythm of the quarter-squares. Press toward the inner border.

13. Add a corner block to each end of both side borders, matching the rhythm of the colors. Press toward the center of the row.

14. Sew the side borders to the quilt top, matching the cream diamonds and the color rhythm of the quarter-squares. The quilt top will measure 94½" × 94½".

Finishing

1. Layer, baste, and quilt as desired.

2. Add binding (page 16).

Quilt assembly

Sisters

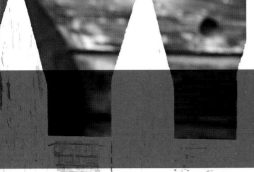

And those who were seen dancing were thought to be insane by those who could not hear the music.

—*Friedrich Nietzsche*

Sisters Wallhanging

Finished blocks: Flying Geese: 3″ × 6″ • Square-in-a-Square: 6″ × 6″
Finished wallhanging: 50″ × 69″

The first project in the Sisters design series, also known as *Tribal Dance*, is a column quilt with top and bottom borders. It was designed to showcase the uniqueness of its fabrics, and it is *all* about the fabric! The two primary fabrics are hand-stamped artisan batiks with large-scale dominant prints that I saw as Flying Geese. They have a soft hand and an irregular appearance. I combined them with some of their companions in the line but then added contrasting textures. These prints are cut lengthwise, parallel to the selvage, so be sure to take the direction of the print into consideration when making your fabric selections.

The only true piecing in the quilt is in the three columns, with leftover half-square triangle units combining for the pieced borders. Controlling the background color of the Flying Geese blocks gives the illusion of vertical ribbons behind the triangles, and contrasting textures and shine do all the work in creating added dimension and interest. This project is a great example of playing with eclectics. It also illustrates how the fabrics do the work and the pattern is at times secondary.

Read Exploring New Textiles: Eclectic Fabric Guidelines (page 6) before beginning.

Note: Interface all the silk dupioni before cutting. Also test any other loose weaves to determine whether they would benefit from interfacing before you begin.

TIP • When using wool in the piecing of projects, I do not typically interface it. But by the nature of its fiber and weave, wool can have some stretch. When it is designed into the body of a quilt and sewn on all sides, there is not much of a stability issue. In this project, wool is used as the outer top and bottom border. Seaming will not be an issue, but if you intend to have the wallhanging quilted by a longarm quilter, I would encourage you to put a lightweight interfacing on it before cutting to minimize stretching during quilting. It is not a requirement but rather something that my quilter and I thought might be a good idea. Just be sure to keep the interfacing light in weight so that you will still benefit from the loft you get when quilting wool.

Materials

Focal batik prints in 2 contrasting colorways—green *and* gray: 1⅝ yards *each* for columns, piecing, and binding

Mixed batiks: 1 fat eighth (9″ × 20″) *each* of 8 coordinating colors for Flying Geese blocks

Radiance silk/cotton blends: 1 fat quarter (18″ × 20″) or ¼ yard *each* of 3 coordinating colors for Flying Geese and Square-in-a-Square blocks

Gray silk dupioni: ⅓ yard for border

Olive-green silk dupioni: ⅓ yard for border

Turquoise wool (at least 52″ wide): ½ yard for border

Interfacing for silks

Backing: 3¼ yards

Binding: ⅝ yard (*included in yardage at left*)

Batting: 58″ × 72″

Cutting

To ensure the best results, make sure that all the fabrics are first pressed well and free from folds or wrinkles. Prepare the fabrics as needed by referring to Exploring New Textiles: Eclectic Fabric Guidelines (page 6).

FOCAL BATIK PRINTS

From *each* of the 2 prints:

• Cut 1 strip 10½″ × 45½″ on the lengthwise grain.

• Cut 1 strip 6½″ × 45½″ on the lengthwise grain.

• Cut 4 strips 3½″ × length of fabric; subcut 50 squares 3½″ × 3½″. Use the extra fabric left over after cutting the 10½″ and 6½″ strips to cut some squares if needed.

• Cut 3 strips 2½″ × length of fabric for the binding.

MIXED BATIKS

• Cut 4 strips 3½″ × 6½″ from *each* of the 8 batiks.

RADIANCE SILK/COTTON BLENDS

• Cut 4 strips 3½″ × 6½″ from *each* of the 3 fabrics for the Flying Geese blocks.

• Cut 1 square 6½″ × 6½″ from *each* of the 3 fabrics for the Square-in-a-Square blocks.

GRAY SILK DUPIONI

• Cut 3 strips 1½″ × width of fabric.

OLIVE-GREEN SILK DUPIONI

• Cut 3 strips 1½″ × width of fabric.

TURQUOISE WOOL

• Cut 2 strips 6½″ × 50½″.

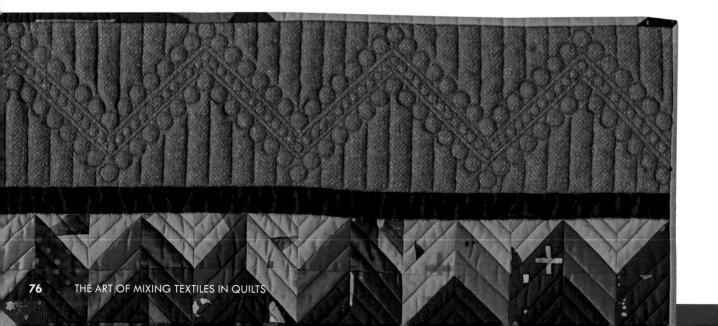

Construction

Sew all the seams with an accurate ¼″ seam allowance. The fabrics should be paired and sewn right sides together. Follow the pressing instructions in the diagrams, and press consistently throughout the construction process. These instructions will help you achieve opposing seam conditions and make for a flatter quilt face.

The seams should be pressed on the right side of the blocks. With the silks, take care that your iron is not too hot; do a test sample first. Press from the back if necessary or use a pressing cloth. Consult Exploring New Textiles: Eclectic Fabric Guidelines (page 6).

The Flying Geese blocks in this project are made in the traditional way: by layering squares onto strips, stitching from corner to corner, and trimming away the excess. Using the two contrasting focal prints as the "sky" fabric in each block creates the illusion of vertical stripes behind the geese. To achieve this illusion, as well as to maintain the rhythm of the contrasting bands in the finished quilt, it is important to control the color placement.

FLYING GEESE BLOCKS

1. Draw a diagonal line from corner to corner on the wrong side of each 3½″ green focal batik square. Layer a marked square on the upper *right* corner of a 3½″ × 6½″ mixed batik or Radiance strip. Stitch on the drawn line.

2. Draw a parallel line a scant ½″ from the sewn line. Sew on this second line and cut between the lines of stitching. Press the seams toward the green focal batik. *The cutaway half-square triangle unit is a dividend! Set this aside, as it will be used later in the pieced borders. You will also have 6 extra focal batik squares, which will be used later.*

3. Draw a diagonal line from corner to corner on the wrong side of each 3½″ gray focal batik square. Layer a marked square on the upper *left* corner of a unit made in Step 2. Stitch on the drawn line.

4. Draw a parallel line a scant ½″ from the sewn line. Sew on this second line and cut between the lines of stitching. Press the seams toward the gray focal batik. *Set aside the cutaway half-square triangle units for the pieced borders. You will also have 6 extra focal batik squares, which will be used later.*

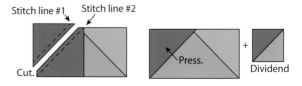

5. The Flying Geese blocks will measure 3½″ × 6½″. Make 44. You will have 5 extra geese but the right number of dividends for the pieced borders.

6. Trim all the dividend half-square triangle units to 2½″ × 2½″. You will have 44 with the green focal batik and 44 with the gray focal batik.

SQUARE-IN-A-SQUARE BLOCKS

1. Layer a marked 3½″ green focal batik square on the upper right corner of a 6½″ Radiance square. Layer a marked 3½″ gray focal batik square on the lower left corner of the same Radiance square. Sew from corner to corner on the drawn diagonal lines.

2. Draw a parallel line a scant ½″ away from each of the sewn lines. Stitch on the lines.

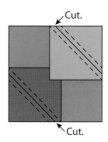

3. Cut away the half-square triangle units. Press toward the focal batiks, and trim the units to 2½″ × 2½″. *More dividends!*

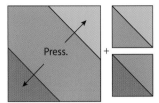

4. Layer a marked 3½″ green square on the lower right corner and a marked 3½″ gray square on the upper left corner of the layered square sewn in Step 3. Sew from corner to corner on the drawn diagonal lines.

5. Draw a parallel line a scant ½″ away from each of the sewn lines. Stitch on the lines.

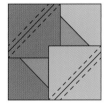

6. Cut away the half-square triangle units. Press toward the focal batiks, and trim the units to 2½″ × 2½″. *2 additional dividends!*

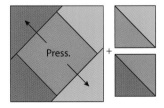

7. The Square-in-a-Square blocks will measure 6½″ × 6½″. Make 3. You will have 12 additional half-square triangle units—6 with the green focal batik and 6 with the gray. There are now 100 half-square triangle units. Set these aside for the pieced borders.

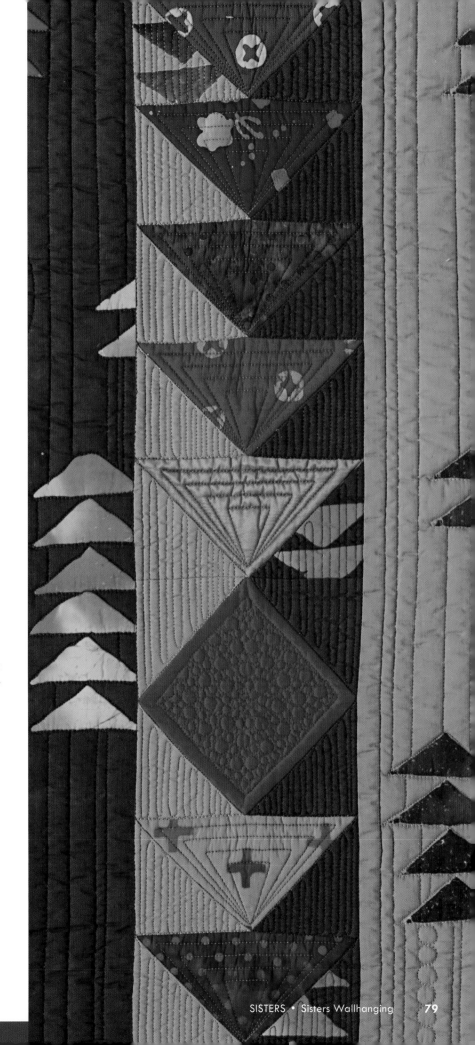

Quilt Assembly

1. A pieced column consists of 14 blocks: 1 Square-in-a-Square block and 13 Flying Geese blocks. All the geese should be pointed in the same direction. Press the seams in each column in one direction. The column will measure 6½″ × 45½″. Make 3 columns.

TIP • Position the Square-in-a-Square blocks within the columns so that they are scattered evenly throughout the quilt top. This is an old art-school trick that helps your eye travel through the project as it picks up the lightest, or in this case shiniest, points and draws your eye's attention. These Square-in-a-Square blocks also interrupt the expected pattern of Flying Geese blocks, making the layout more interesting and giving your eye a place to rest.

2. Referring to the quilt assembly diagram, sew together the following pieces, working from left to right:

6½″ × 45½″ green focal batik strip

6½″ × 45½″ pieced column, with the geese flying up

10½″ × 45½″ gray focal batik strip

6½″ × 45½″ pieced column, with the geese flying down

10½″ × 45½″ green focal batik strip

6½″ × 45½″ pieced column, with the geese flying up

6½″ × 45½″ gray focal batik strip

3. Press the seams toward the focal batiks. The quilt top will now measure 45½″ × 50½″.

4. Sew together the 3 olive-green silk dupioni 1½″ × width of fabric strips end to end. Subcut 2 strips 1½″ × 50½″. Sew these strips to the top and bottom of the quilt top. Press toward the silk strips.

5. The second border is made up of half-square triangle units, but you have already done all the piecing. It is here where you will use the *dividends*! Having sewn the Flying Geese blocks by adding both a green and a gray focal batik square to each strip, you now have pairs of half-square triangle units. Each pair shares the same goose fabric, but one has a green half and one has a gray half. Assemble 50 pairs, as shown: 25 pairs will be *left-handed* and 25 pairs will be *right-handed*. Sew the pairs together. Each unit will be 2½″ × 4½″.

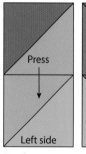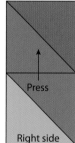

Border pairs

6. Sew together 2 border rows using 25 pairs in each row. Alternate the *left*- and *right*-handed pairs to create the chevron pattern. The rows will measure 4½″ × 50½″. Press in one direction.

Border

7. Add one pieced horizontal border to the top of your quilt top and the other to the bottom. Orient the borders so that the gray halves of the half-square triangle units are sewn to the olive-green silk dupioni border. Press toward the silk border.

8. Sew together the 3 gray silk dupioni 1½″ × width of fabric strips end to end. Subcut 2 strips 1½″ × 50½″. Sew these strips to the top and bottom of the quilt top. Press toward the silk strips.

9. Sew the 6½″ × 50½″ turquoise wool strips to the top and bottom of the quilt top. Press toward the silk border.

Finishing

1. Layer, baste, and quilt as desired.

2. Add binding (page 16).

> ***Note:*** *Notice that the columns start with a green vertical strip on the left-hand side of the quilt and end with a gray vertical strip on the right-hand side of the quilt. The binding is cut from these same two fabrics. I wanted the binding strips to contrast with these edges as they wrap around the project, so the left side has the contrasting gray binding and the right side has the contrasting green binding. As you join your strips, anticipate where the color will need to change to achieve this contrast.*

Quilt assembly

Sisters Throw

Finished blocks: Flying Geese: 3″ × 6″ • Square-in-a-Square: 6″ × 6″
Finished throw: 54″ × 66″

The *Sisters Throw* is the second sister, also known as *Jitterbug*. The two sisters are born of the same "parents" but dance to the beat of their own drummers. The *Sisters Throw* takes its cues from the unique manner in which the fabric was printed. It's a simple pattern with very little piecing, but it has strong graphic impact. It is a bit different from *Tribal Dance* in its orientation. Unlike *Tribal Dance*, it has only columns, with no horizontal components.

Bordered prints are often difficult to incorporate into quilt projects, and this graded focal print from Handcrafted by Alison Glass was no exception. It is printed in an ombré manner. The heaviest density of printing occurs near the selvage and fades to the middle from both sides. It would lend itself to piecing by giving a diversity of print options to the various cuts, but I thought for this one I'd let the fabric speak. I used a large cut to showcase the printing and then pieced only the middle.

Listen to your fabrics. Sometimes they sing, sometimes they are somber, and sometimes they scream for attention. Listen … who knows what dance their song will lead you to?

Read Exploring New Textiles: Eclectic Fabric Guidelines (page 6) before beginning.

Materials

Hand-stamped gray ombré focal batik print: 2 yards for body

Green batik: ¼ yard for block backgrounds

Gray batik: ¼ yard for block backgrounds

Mixed batiks: ¼ yard *each* of 8 coordinating colors for Flying Geese blocks, appliquéd circles, and columns (You can use fat quarters [18″ × 20″] for 4 of these fabrics.)

Radiance silk/cotton blends: 1 fat eighth (9″ × 20″) *each* of 3 coordinating colors for Flying Geese and Square-in-a-Square blocks

Backing: 3½ yards

Binding: ⅝ yard

Batting: 62″ × 74″

Cutting

To ensure the best results, make sure that all the fabrics are first pressed well and free from folds or wrinkles. Prepare the fabrics as needed by referring to Exploring New Textiles: Eclectic Fabric Guidelines (page 6).

HAND-STAMPED GRAY OMBRÉ FOCAL BATIK PRINT

• Cut 2 strips 20½″ × 66½″ on the lengthwise grain.

GREEN BATIK

• Cut 22 squares 3½″ × 3½″.

GRAY BATIK

• Cut 22 squares 3½″ × 3½″.

MIXED BATIKS

• Cut a total of 13 strips 3½″ × 6½″ for the Flying Geese.

• Cut a total of 4 strips 2½″ × 21½″ for the pieced columns (A).

• Cut a total of 4 strips 2½″ × 15½″ for the pieced columns (B).

• Cut a total of 20 strips 2½″ × 6½″ for the pieced columns (C).

• Cut 3 circles 4½″ in diameter for the Square-in-a-Square blocks, using the pattern (page 85).

RADIANCE SILK/COTTON BLENDS

• Cut 1 square 6½″ × 6½″ from *each* of the 3 fabrics for the Square-in-a-Square blocks.

• Cut 1 strip 3½″ × 6½″ from *each* of the 3 fabrics for the Flying Geese blocks.

BINDING

• Cut 7 strips 2½″ × width of fabric.

Pieced by Teresa Kasch

Construction

Sew all the seams with an accurate ¼" *seam allowance. The fabrics should be paired and sewn right sides together. Follow the pressing instructions in the diagrams, and press consistently throughout the construction process. These instructions will help you achieve opposing seam conditions and make for a flatter quilt face.*

The seams should be pressed on the right side of the blocks. With the silk blends, take care that your iron is not too hot; do a test sample first. Press from the back if necessary or use a pressing cloth. Consult Exploring New Textiles: Eclectic Fabric Guidelines (page 6).

The Flying Geese blocks in this project are made traditionally by layering squares onto strips, stitching from corner to corner, and trimming away the excess. Using the contrasting green and gray batiks as the "sky" in each block creates the illusion of a vertical stripe behind the geese. To achieve this illusion, it is important to control the color placement. Use a design wall to visualize the direction your geese are flying in.

FLYING GEESE BLOCKS

1. Draw a diagonal line from corner to corner on the wrong side of each 3½" green batik square. On 6 mixed batik 3½" × 6½" strips, layer a marked green square on the upper *right* corner. These geese will fly *up*. On the remaining 7 mixed batik 3½" × 6½" strips, layer a square on the upper *left* corner. These geese will fly *down*. Stitch on the drawn lines.

2. Draw a parallel line a scant ½" from the sewn line. Sew on this second line and cut between the lines of stitching. Press the seams toward the green batik. *The cutaway half-square triangle unit is a dividend! Set this aside to use for another project.*

> **Note:** *See the Dividend projects (page 98) for ideas on how to use the dividends from this project (leftover half-square triangle units).*

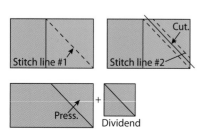

3. Draw a diagonal line from corner to corner on the wrong side of each 3½" gray batik square. Layer a gray square on the upper *left* corner of each strip made in Step 1 that is flying *up* and on the upper *right* corner of each strip made in Step 1 that is flying *down*. Stitch on the drawn lines. Follow Step 2 to create more dividend half-square triangle units.

4. Press toward the gray batik. The Flying Geese blocks will measure 3½" × 6½". Make 13: 6 flying up and 7 flying down.

5. Repeat this process with the remaining 3½" green and gray squares and the 3½" × 6½" Radiance strips. Make 3 Flying Geese blocks: 2 flying up and 1 flying down.

SQUARE-IN-A-SQUARE BLOCKS

1. Layer a marked 3½" green batik square on the upper *right* corner of each 6½" Radiance square. Layer a marked 3½" gray batik square on the lower *left* corner of each Radiance square. Sew from corner to corner on the drawn diagonal lines. Follow Flying Geese Blocks, Step 2 to create more dividend half-square triangle units. Press toward the batiks.

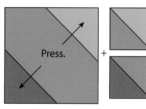

2. Layer a 3½" green batik square on the lower *right* corner and a 3½" gray batik square on the upper *left* corner of the layered squares sewn in Step 1. Sew from corner to corner on the drawn lines. You can make more dividend half-square triangle units in this step, too! Press toward the batiks.

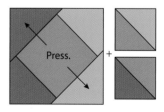

3. Appliqué a 4"-diameter circle in the center of each of the blocks. I machine appliquéd these circles in place, but you can certainly use the appliqué method of your choice.

4. The Square-in-a-Square blocks will measure 6½" × 6½". Make 3.

Quilt Assembly

1. The center column consists of 19 blocks: 3 Square-in-a-Square blocks and 16 Flying Geese blocks. Referring to the center assembly diagram, sew the blocks together. Press all the seams in one direction. The column will measure 6½″ × 66½″.

2. The A, B, and C strips cut from the mixed batiks are sewn together in 2 column configurations: outer and inner. Sew the strips together end to end and top to bottom. Make 2 outer columns and 2 inner columns, referring to the quilt assembly diagram. The columns will each measure 2½″ × 66½″.

Press the seams of each column in alternating directions.

  Outer columns: A, C, C, C, C, A

  Inner columns: C, C, C, B, B, C, C, C

3. Join the 5 columns from right to left.

4. Add 20½″ × 66½″ focal print strips to the left and right sides of the quilt center.

> **Note:** *Take notice of the density of the print in the focal fabric. Align both the outside/selvage edges, which have the greater print density, with the quilt center.*

5. Press the seams away from the center. The quilt top will measure 54½″ × 66½″.

Finishing

1. Layer, baste, and quilt as desired.

2. Add binding (page 16).

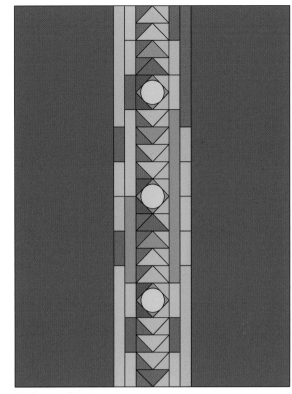

Quilt assembly

Center assembly

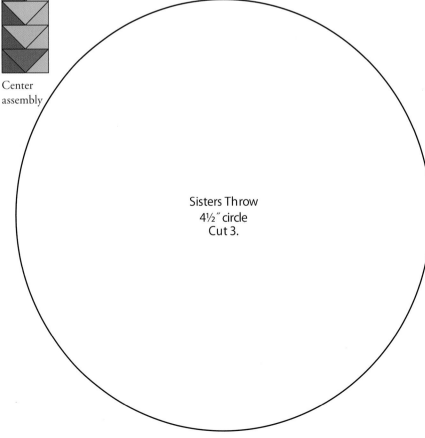

Sisters Throw
4½″ circle
Cut 3.

Echoes of Italy

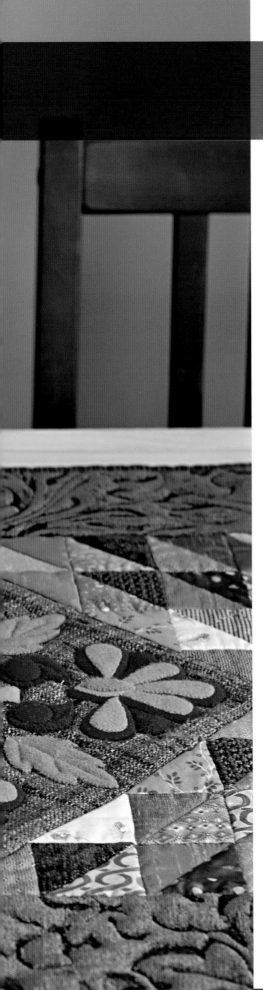

Echoes of Italy Table Runner

Finished Birds in the Air blocks: 8″ × 8″
Finished table runner: 24″ × 72″

Echoes of Italy's inspiration is from the past. It is a mixed-medium textiles project that uses 23 different fabrics with multiple textures and weaves. Project fabrics included 2 silk dupionis, silk matka, Radiance silk/cotton blends, 5 varying grades of home decor textiles, a batik, and 8 traditional cottons. Echoes can be constructed as either a bolster or a runner. The palette is drawn from the rolling hills of Italy at dusk.

I have long been intrigued by the patterns in the floors, windows, and architectural details throughout Europe. Echoes of Italy's appliqué motif was inspired by the Cathedral of Santa Maria Assunta in Italy. The almost feather-like quality of the appliqué design was inspired by a motif found in the tile patterns and the ornamentation that can be found throughout the cathedral. The use of the Birds in the Air blocks is evocative of the mosaic floors of the Basilica di Santa Maria Maggiore in Rome. By incorporating the leaves into the body of the project and appliquéing them off the traditional "background" of the central medallion, I was mimicking yet another architectural detail: a carved soffit or cornice. Marrying it all together surely is an echo of Italy.

Read Exploring New Textiles: Eclectic Fabric Guidelines (page 6) before beginning.

Floor tile in Cathedral of Santa Maria Assunta, Italy

Materials

FABRICS FOR BLOCKS AND BORDER

Mixed-medium fabrics: 1¼ yards *total* of 18 fabrics for half-square triangles (Each piece should measure at least 3″ × 27″ or 6″ × 14″.)

Green plaid wool (54″–60″ wide): ½ yard for Birds in the Air blocks (If your fabric is wider than 56″, you will need only ¼ yard.)

Bronze textured silk matka: 1 fat quarter (18″ × 20″) *or* ½ yard for appliqué background

Brown chenille upholstery: 2 yards, cut lengthwise, for borders without seams *or* ¾ yard, cut across the width of fabric, for borders with seams

HAND-DYED WOOL FOR APPLIQUÉ

Garnet, dark plum, *and* seal brown: 8″ × 10″ *each* for medallion

Gold: 6″ × 8″ for medallion and small oval accents

Green: Approximately 8″ × 22″ for leaves

OTHER MATERIALS

Interfacing for hand-dyed wools and silks

Color-coordinated wool thread for appliqué

Backing: 1½ yards

Binding: ½ yard

Batting: 32″ × 80″

Cutting

MIXED-MEDIUM FABRICS

- From *each* of the 18 fabrics, cut 7 squares 2⅞″ × 2⅞″ for the pieced triangle blocks. Cut 1 additional square 2⅞″ × 2⅞″ from one of the fabrics.

  Choose 32 of the lighter-weight squares and cut in half diagonally.

GREEN PLAID WOOL

- Cut 6 squares 8⅞″ × 8⅞″; cut in half diagonally.

BRONZE TEXTURED SILK MATKA

- Cut 1 square 14″ × 14″.

BROWN CHENILLE UPHOLSTERY

- Cut 2 strips 4½″ × 64½″. They can be cut on the lengthwise grain *or* pieced from 3 or 4 strips 4½″ × width of fabric.

- Cut 2 strips 4½″ × 24½″.

BINDING

- Cut 5 strips 2½″ × width of fabric.

TIPS

- To improve accuracy, you can cut the mixed-medium squares for the half-square triangle units 3″ × 3″ and trim them down after sewing.

- The heaviest of the home decor fabrics will be the hardest to press adjacent to the wool. Don't cut these diagonally.

Construction

All seam allowances are ¼" unless otherwise noted. Fabrics are paired right sides together. Prepare all the fabrics before you cut; refer to Exploring New Textiles: Eclectic Fabric Guidelines (page 6). Interface all silks and unstable weaves.

HALF-SQUARE TRIANGLE UNITS

There are many ways to construct half-square triangle units. What follows is a traditional method. The focus of this project is to make the units scrappy; you do not need to worry about a light/dark rhythm in the pairing of the fabrics, although some contrast is encouraged. Pair them based on both color and weight. Avoid putting two heavy fabrics together—weight is a greater issue than fiber content when piecing with eclectics. How fabrics will press is actually the first consideration when pairing. How they come together in the block is secondary.

1. Choose at least 48 pairs of 2 squares each from the 2⅞" mixed-medium squares. If you use more squares, you'll have more choices when you assemble the table runner, with some left over for another project. Draw a diagonal line from corner to corner on the wrong side of the lighter-weight, smoother-textured square of each pair.

2. Layer the squares of each pair right sides together and sew ¼" on each side of the drawn line.

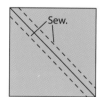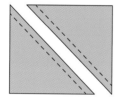

Half-square triangle units

TIP • A walking foot or even-feed foot is helpful for some of the heavier textures but is not mandatory. By pairing a cotton with a specialty fabric and drawing the diagonal line on the cotton, you will be feeding the pair through your machine with the specialty fabric on the bed of the machine. This helps with both nap issues and stretch.

3. Cut on the drawn line and press. Traditionally, we press away from light-colored fabrics. In eclectics, press away from the heavier of the 2 fabrics you have paired. In the case of the home decor textiles, you may have greater success pressing the seams open.

4. The half-square triangle units will measure 2½" × 2½". Make 96.

BIRDS IN THE AIR BLOCKS

The Birds in the Air blocks are assembled using the mixed-medium half-square triangles and the green plaid wool triangles. The intent is to have these blocks read scrappy. Light and dark color placement does not need to be consistent, but, as always, the decision is yours to make. Half of this block is solid, and half is pieced from the 2½" half-square triangle units and the diagonally cut triangles. You will assemble sixteen large pieced triangles for your project; twelve will be combined with the green plaid wool triangles to complete the Birds in the Air blocks, and four will surround the appliquéd background.

1. For each pieced triangle, select 6 mixed-medium half-square triangle units and 4 mixed-medium triangles. Arrange the units and triangles in 4 rows, following the pieced triangle assembly diagram.

Row 1: 3 half-square triangle units and 1 triangle

Row 2: 2 half-square triangle units and 1 triangle

Row 3: 1 half-square triangle unit and 1 triangle

Row 4: 1 triangle

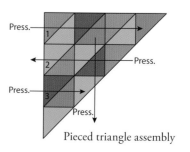

Pieced triangle assembly

2. Using a walking foot or even-feed foot, sew the units together in rows. Press the rows in alternating directions.

3. Sew the rows together as shown. Press the seams toward the block centerline. Once all 16 of the pieced triangles are assembled, set aside 4 for use around the appliqué background, and finish the assembly of the Birds in the Air blocks.

4. Sew together 1 green plaid wool triangle and 1 large pieced triangle. Place the pieced triangle on top of the wool as you feed it through your machine. The wool will be on the bed of the machine. This will allow you to see and control the joins on the pieced section as you sew *and* help in minimizing the stretch of the wool.

5. The block will measure 8½″ × 8½″. Make 12.

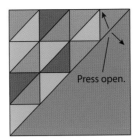

Birds in the Air block

Appliqué

Refer to Wool Appliqué … My Way (page 12).

1. Prepare the appliqué pieces in the quantities indicated using the project patterns (page 93).

TIP • For the circles, I sometimes draw directly onto the freezer paper with an architectural circle template, a tool left over in my crayon box from my first design life! You may prefer to do the same.

> *Note: The textured silk matka used for the appliqué background has a looser weave than many silks. It would benefit from being stabilized with a lightweight interfacing like Touch O'Gold II. I chose the black version of this interfacing so that the color would not be seen on the face of the finished project.*

2. Prepare the background square. The 14″ bronze textured silk matka square is oversize. To ensure that your appliqué will fall well within the trim area, mark the 12″ × 12″ trim line with either chalk or a line of hand-basted stitching in contrasting thread. Textured silk matka does tend to fray. Zigzag the edges on your machine or stabilize with the method of your choice before you begin the appliqué work.

3. Find the center of the block. Following the project photographs, lay out all the appliqué medallion pieces.

4. Appliqué the feathers, starburst points, and circles, working from the center out.

5. Re-center your design within the 12″ × 12″ design area, if necessary, and trim the appliquéd background to 11¾″ × 11¾″. The remaining leaves and circles in the body of the project will be appliquéd after the blocks are joined together.

Assembly

1. Add the 4 remaining pieced triangles to the appliquéd medallion background. Refer to the appliqué block assembly diagram. The background is now *on point*. Depending on the weight of the fabrics in the seam, press the seams open or toward the center on 2 parallel sides and away from the center on the 2 remaining sides. The completed medallion appliqué block will measure 16½″ × 16½″.

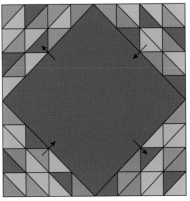

Appliqué block assembly

2. Join the 12 Birds in the Air blocks into 6 columns of 2 blocks each. Rotate the blocks so that they are oriented as shown.

Note: The appliquéd block was intentionally offset from the center in this project.

Table runner assembly

3. Sew the columns together as shown. Press the joining seams open.

TIP • I have discovered that an old-fashioned tailor's tool called a clapper is a great asset for pressing wool and home decor seams open. The result is flatter and more stabilized seams, making for a much smoother project face. Why it works is pure science and beyond my ability to explain, but it has to do with the combination of the porousness of the wood tool, steam, and pressure. The Steady Betty offers a version of it that works really well, too.

4. Appliqué the remaining circles and leaves to the chevron areas created by the secondary patterning of the joined blocks.

5. Sew the 2 brown chenille upholstery 64½″ strips to the long sides of the project. Home decor fabrics like the one I chose have a nap and will tend to move away from the seamline as you sew. Use a walking foot or even-feed foot and place the chenille fabric on the bed of the machine as you stitch. Watch the raw edges to keep them aligned. Press the seams open.

6. Sew the 2 brown chenille upholstery 24½″ strips to the short edges of the project. Press the seams open. The top will measure 24½″ × 72½″.

Note: I am a strong advocate for early thought on the integration of the final quilting of a project. Quilting can be integral to the design of the whole project and does not serve just as a means of holding the three quilt layers together. I wanted the chevron elements of the Echoes of Italy Table Runner *to mirror the lines of carved-wood moldings, and the quilting on our sample delineates those lines. The leaves are appliquéd but could just as easily have been drawn with the quilter's needle.*

Finishing

1. Layer, baste, and quilt as desired.

2. Add binding (page 16).

TIP • Sew the binding strip to the face of the quilt top with a ¼″–⅜″ seam allowance, aligning the raw edges. Due to the thickness of the home decor fabric in the borders, a slightly deeper seam allowance may be beneficial.

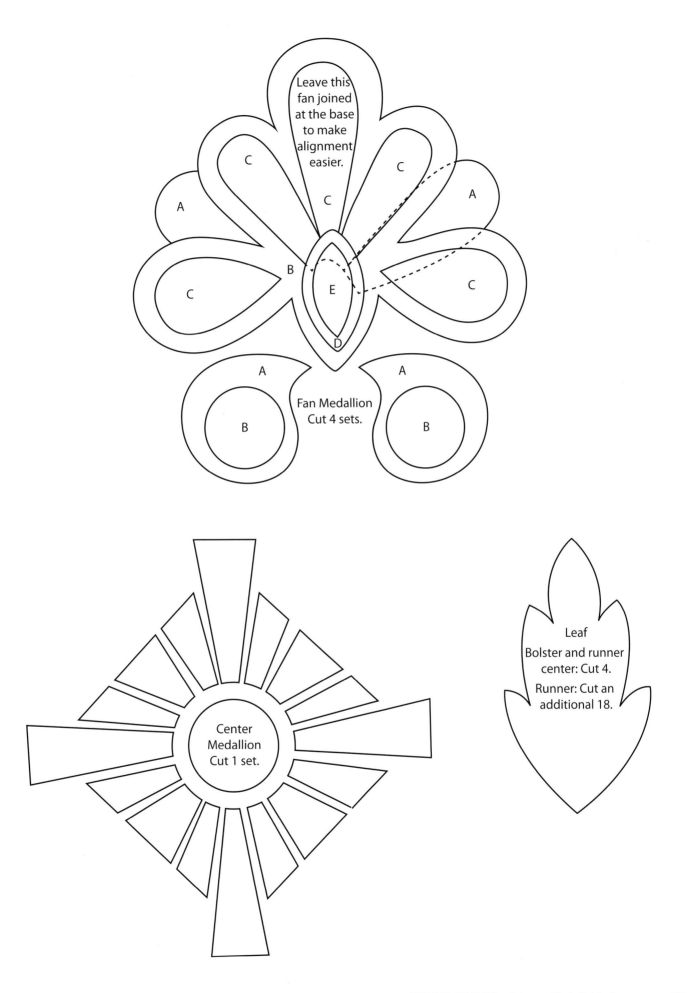

Leave this fan joined at the base to make alignment easier.

C

A

C

C

C

A

B

C

E

C

D

A

A

B

Fan Medallion
Cut 4 sets.

B

Center
Medallion
Cut 1 set.

Leaf
Bolster and runner
center: Cut 4.

Runner: Cut an
additional 18.

Echoes of Italy Bolster

Finished Birds in the Air blocks: *8″ × 8″*
Finished bolster: *20″ × 36″*

The bolster version of Echoes of Italy uses the same Birds in the Air blocks and construction methods as the table runner project. Follow the sewing directions for the runner, but work in the quantities specified below. Note that the yardage needed is not what dictates the mixed-medium fabric requirements. It is the variety. The runner uses eighteen fabrics, but this bolster would have adequate yardage using twelve fabrics. Project fabrics included two silk dupionis, silk matka, Radiance silk/cotton blends, two to five different grades of home decor textiles, a batik, and five to eight traditional cottons. More variation in the fabrics will give you more interest in the finished top. More is better here!

Many eclectic projects lend themselves to embellishment. Sometimes it's embroidery embellishment; sometimes it's beading. The bolster version of this project illustrates a bit of both. Of special note is the background treatment. I used a bead referred to as a peanut bead to add a metallic background texture rather than just a graphic outline for the appliqué.

Read Exploring New Textiles: Eclectic Fabric Guidelines (page 6) before beginning.

Materials

FABRICS FOR BLOCKS AND BORDER

Mixed-medium fabrics: 1¼ yards *total* of 18 fabrics for half-square triangles

Green plaid wool: ⅓ yard for Birds in the Air blocks and border corners

Bronze textured silk matka: 1 fat quarter (18″ × 20″) *or* ½ yard for appliqué background

Brown chenille upholstery: ¼ yard for border

HAND-DYED WOOL FOR APPLIQUÉ

Garnet, dark plum, *and* **seal brown:** 6″ × 8″ *each* for medallion

Gold: 6″ × 8″ for medallion and small circle accents

Green: Approximately 8″ × 22″ for leaves

OTHER MATERIALS

Interfacing for hand-dyed wools and silks

Muslin (at least 40″ wide): ⅔ yard

Polyester fiberfill

Color-coordinated wool thread for appliqué

Backing: ¾ yard

Batting: 28″ × 44″

Embroidery threads *(optional)*

Accent beads *(optional)*

Cutting

MIXED-MEDIUM FABRICS

• From *each* of the 18 fabrics, cut 3 squares 2⅞″ × 2⅞″ for the pieced triangle units. Cut 10 additional squares 2⅞″ × 2⅞″.

Choose 16 of the lighter-weight squares and cut in half diagonally.

GREEN PLAID WOOL

• Cut 2 squares 8⅞″ × 8⅞″; cut in half diagonally.

• Cut 4 squares 2½″ × 2½″.

BRONZE TEXTURED SILK MATKA

• Cut 1 square 14″ × 14″.

BROWN CHENILLE UPHOLSTERY

• Cut 2 strips 2½″ × 32½″.

• Cut 2 strips 2½″ × 16½″.

MUSLIN

• Cut 1 piece 28″ × width of fabric.

BACKING

• Cut 1 piece 20½″ × 36½″.

Construction

All seam allowances are ¼″ unless otherwise noted. Fabrics are paired right sides together. Prepare all the fabrics before you cut; refer to Exploring New Textiles: Eclectic Fabric Guidelines (page 6). Interface all silks and unstable weaves.

HALF-SQUARE TRIANGLE UNITS

Refer to Echoes of Italy Table Runner, *Half-Square Triangle Units (page 90).*

1. Choose 24 pairs of 2 squares each from the 2⅞″ mixed-medium squares. Draw a diagonal line from corner to corner on the wrong side of the lighter-weight square of each pair.

2. Layer the squares of each pair right sides together and sew ¼″ on each side of the drawn line.

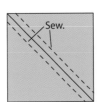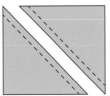

Half-square triangle units

TIP • A walking foot or even-feed foot is helpful for some of the heavier textures but is not mandatory. By pairing a cotton with a specialty fabric and drawing the diagonal line on the cotton, you will be feeding the pair through your machine with the specialty fabric on the bed of the machine. This helps with both nap issues and stretch.

3. Cut on the drawn line and press open. Traditionally, we press away from light-color fabrics. In eclectics, press away from the heavier of the 2 fabrics you have paired. In the case of the home decor textiles, you may have greater success pressing the seams open.

4. The half-square triangle units will measure 2½″ × 2½″. Make 48.

BIRDS IN THE AIR BLOCKS

The Birds in the Air blocks are assembled using the mixed-medium half-square triangles and the green plaid wool triangles. The intent is to have these blocks read scrappy. Light and dark color placement does not need to be consistent, but, as always, the decision is yours to make. Half of this block is solid, and half is pieced from the 2½″ half-square triangle units and the diagonally cut triangles. You will assemble eight large pieced triangles for your project; four will be combined with the green plaid wool triangles to complete the Birds in the Air blocks, and four will surround the appliquéd background.

1. For each pieced triangle, select 6 mixed-medium half-square triangle units and 4 mixed-medium triangles. Arrange the triangle units and triangles in 4 rows following the pieced triangle assembly diagram.

    Row 1: 3 half-square triangle units and 1 triangle

    Row 2: 2 half-square triangle units and 1 triangle

    Row 3: 1 half-square triangle unit and 1 triangle

    Row 4: 1 triangle

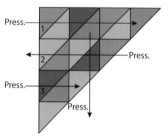

Pieced triangle assembly

2. Using a walking foot or even-feed foot, sew the units together in rows. Press the rows in alternating directions.

3. Sew the rows together as shown, and press the seams toward the block centerline. Once all 8 of the pieced triangles are assembled, set aside 4 for use around the appliqué background, and finish the assembly of the Birds in the Air blocks.

4. Sew together 1 green plaid wool triangle and 1 large pieced triangle. Place the pieced triangle on top of the wool as you feed it through your machine. The wool will be on the bed of the machine. This will allow you to see and control the joins on the pieced section as you sew *and* help in minimizing the stretch of the wool.

5. The block will measure 8½″ × 8½″. Make 4.

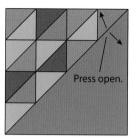

Birds in the Air block

Appliqué

Refer to Wool Appliqué … My Way (page 12).

1. Prepare the appliqué pieces in the quantities indicated using the project patterns (page 93).

TIP • For the circles, I sometimes draw directly onto the freezer paper with an architectural circle template, a tool left over in my crayon box from my first design life! You may prefer to do the same.

Note: The textured silk matka used for the appliqué background has a looser weave than many silks. It would benefit from being stabilized with a lightweight interfacing like Touch O'Gold II. I chose the black version of this interfacing so that the color would not be seen on the face of the finished project.

2. Refer to *Echoes of Italy Table Runner*, Appliqué (page 91) to appliqué, re-center, and trim the background silk matka square.

3. If desired, embellish your project with embroidery before it is sewn together with the pieced blocks. The embroidery threads I used are all from Wonderfil. Refer to Embroidery (page 18).

Assembly

1. Add the 4 remaining pieced trian-gles to the appliquéd medallion back-ground. Refer to the appliqué block assembly diagram. The background is now *on point*. Depending on the weight of the fabrics in the seam, press the seams open or toward the center on 2 parallel sides and away from the center on the 2 remaining sides. The completed appliqué block will now measure 16½″ × 16½″.

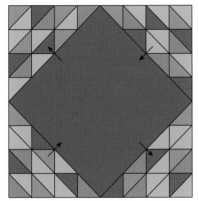

Appliqué block assembly

Appliqué

TIP • Add beads *after* the top has been quilted but *before* it is assembled into the bolster. It is much easier to quilt the top freely without the beads in place, and this also eliminates the chance that the beading threads will be caught by the machine and broken.

2. Join the 4 Birds in the Air blocks into 2 columns of 2 blocks each. Rotate the blocks so that they are oriented as shown in the bolster assembly diagram.

Note: The medallion appliqué block is centered in this project.

3. Sew the columns together as shown. Press the joining seams open.

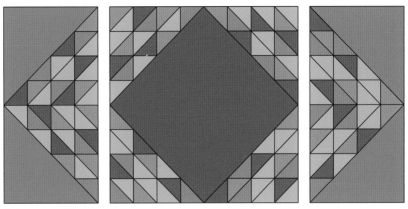

Bolster assembly

4. Sew the 2 brown chenille upholstery 32½″ strips to the top and bottom of the project. Press the seams open.

5. Sew the 2½″ green plaid wool squares to each end of the 16½″ brown chenille upholstery strips. Add the pieced side borders to the project. Press the seams open. The top will measure 20½″ × 36½″.

Finishing

1. Sandwich the batting between the bolster top and muslin. Quilt as desired. Trim to 20½″ × 36½″.

2. Add beading to your project, if desired (see Beading, page 20).

3. Layer the finished top and the 20½″ × 36½″ backing piece, right sides together. Stitch around the entire perimeter of the piece with a ¼″ seam allowance, leaving an opening large enough to turn the bolster right side out. Clip the corners and turn.

4. Stuff lightly with polyester fiberfill and hand stitch the opening closed.

TIP • Do not overstuff. This may cause the pillow to be overly round and lofty, thereby making the appliqué less visible when displayed.

Dividends

THE ART OF MIXING TEXTILES IN QUILTS

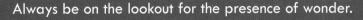

Always be on the lookout for the presence of wonder.

—E. B. White

Dividends Pincushion

Finished pincushion: *6″ × 6″*

A dividend, by definition, is the profit earned on owned shares. The projects here represent the same kind of idea but in quilting terms. When you create a half-square triangle unit by stitching a diagonal line from corner to corner on a square, the next instruction *traditionally* would be to trim the fabric ¼″ away and discard it. Since I work with costly higher-end fabrics, this seemed an incredible waste.

I used a connecting-corner construction in Bohemian Dance, but rather than trimming out the fabric beneath and disposing of it, I sewed an additional parallel line of stitching ½″ away from the first stitched line and cut between the two lines. What results is an additional half-square triangle unit—a dividend! The sizes may be a bit irregular, but they can be trimmed. Bohemian Dance yielded two sizes of dividends: a half-square triangle unit that could be trimmed to finish at 2″ × 2″ and another smaller unit that, when trimmed, finished at ¾″ × ¾″. You can construct the half-square triangle units featured in these projects in any number of ways, but I used the leftovers from Bohemian Dance.

Read Exploring New Textiles: Eclectic Fabric Guidelines (page 6) before beginning.

Note: Interface all the silk dupioni before cutting. Also test any loose weaves to determine whether they would benefit from interfacing before you begin.

Back

Materials

Mixed eclectic blend of textile scraps: Silk dupioni, silk matka, silk/cotton blends, batiks, and mixed cottons for half-square triangle units *or* 36 smaller dividend units

Brown wool flannel: 1 fat eighth (9″ × 21″) or ¼ yard for borders and pincushion back

Decorative ribbon (1½″ wide): 8″ length

Bias-covered small cording with seam allowance: 1 yard

Crushed walnut shells and lavender *or* material of your choice to fill pincushion

Cutting

ECLECTIC SCRAPS

• Trim 36 of the smaller dividend units into 1¼″ × 1¼″ half-square triangle units *or* cut 36 squares 1⅝″ × 1⅝″.

BROWN WOOL FLANNEL

• Cut 2 strips 1¼″ × 5″.

• Cut 2 strips 1¼″ × 6½″.

• Cut 1 square 6½″ × 6½″.

Construction

If you do not have dividend units, construct the half-square triangle units as instructed below.

HALF-SQUARE TRIANGLE UNITS

1. Draw a diagonal line from corner to corner on the wrong side of 18 eclectic scrap squares.

2. Being mindful of the textile weights, pair these squares with the remaining 18 squares, right sides together. Keep the fabric pairs scrappy.

3. Sew a scant ¼″ seam on either side of each drawn line. Cut on the drawn lines. Each pairing yields 2 half-square triangle units, which will measure 1¼″ × 1¼″.

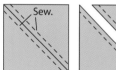

Half-square triangle units

Assembly

1. Organize the 36 half-square triangle units into 6 rows of 6 units each.

2. Sew the rows. Press the rows in alternating directions.

3. Join the rows together. Press in one direction or press the seams open. The top will measure 4½″ × 4½″.

4. Add the 1¼″ × 5″ wool flannel borders to the sides. Press the seams open.

---

5. Add the 1¼″ × 6½″ wool flannel borders to the top and bottom. Press the seams open. The front will measure 6½″ × 6½″.

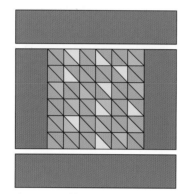

Front assembly

6. Position the length of ribbon on the 6½″ wool flannel square. (I chose to mark a parallel line 1¾″ down from one edge of the back with a chalk marker and to align one edge of the ribbon with this drawn line.) Topstitch the ribbon in place along both long edges.

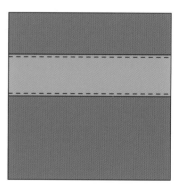

Pincushion back

---

7. Add the cording. Cut a length approximately 30″ long. Pin it to the pincushion top, aligning the raw edges.

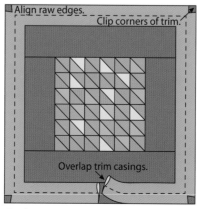

Cord trim

8. Bring the ends together so that they overlap in the middle of one of the sides. Mark the point where they overlap. On *one* of the ends, open the cording fabric and cut just the cord at the point where they meet. Trim the fabric of the cut end approximately 1″ *longer* than where you cut the cord.

9. Fold under the edge of the fabric ½″ on the trimmed end. Align the 2 ends so the interior cords meet but the fabric from the cut end extends beyond the untrimmed end. Wrap the fabric of the cut end around the uncut end, encasing and finishing both edges. Stitch the cording to the pincushion top all the way around using a zipper foot.

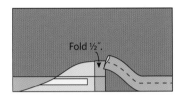

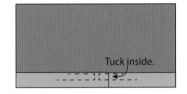

10. Layer the finished top and the back of the pincushion, right sides together. Using a zipper foot, stitch around the entire edge, leaving an opening through which to turn the pincushion right side out.

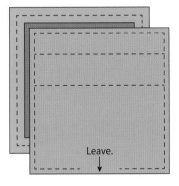

11. Turn the pincushion right side out.

12. Using a funnel, fill the pincushion with the fill of your choice. I used a 70/30 mix of crushed walnut shells and lavender. The walnut shells give it weight, and the lavender lends its lovely scent.

13. Stitch the opening closed by hand.

Dividends Bolster

Finished bolster: 19½″ × 31½″

The *Dividends Bolster* uses both sizes of the half-square triangle units that are by-products of the connecting-corners construction used in Bohemian Dance. Their finished sizes are 2″ × 2″ and ¾″ × ¾″. The larger half-square triangle units are used in the center. A chevron effect is created by controlling the color placement. The smaller half-square triangle units are used as a pieced border. The small size of these half-square triangle units lends a wonderful detail and texture to the project. Wool flannel was used for the solid borders and the back not only to richly frame the brighter-colored detail of the interior but also to create a contrast of texture.

Use your dividends to create this project, or first make the half-square triangle units from yardage. The quantities are given for doing it either way.

Read Exploring New Textiles: Eclectic Fabric Guidelines (page 6) before beginning.

Note: Interface all the silk dupioni before cutting. Also test any other loose weaves to determine whether they would benefit from interfacing before you begin.

Materials

Dividend units: 116 smaller dividend half-square triangle units *and* 72 larger dividend half-square triangle units

Brown wool flannel (54″–60″ wide): ⅓ yard for borders

Backing (54″–60″ wide): ⅝ yard

12″ × 24″ pillow form *or* fiberfill of your choice

If you are constructing the half-square triangle units and *not* using dividend half-square triangle units, you will also need these materials:

Scraps: Approximately ½ yard *total* of mixed eclectic cotton prints

Fuchsia silk matka: ⅛ yard

Teal Radiance silk/cotton blend: ⅛ yard

Turquoise silk dupioni: ⅛ yard

Cutting

DIVIDEND UNITS

- Trim 116 smaller dividend units to 1¼″ × 1¼″.
- Trim 72 larger dividend units to 2½″ × 2½″.

BROWN WOOL FLANNEL

- Cut 2 strips 2″ × 32″.
- Cut 2 strips 2″ × 27½″.
- Cut 2 strips 2″ × 17″.
- Cut 2 strips 2″ × 12½″.

BACKING

- Cut 2 strips 20″ × 22″.

Note: Follow the remaining cutting instructions only if you are not *using dividends from previous projects.*

SCRAPS

- Cut 18 squares 2⅞″ × 2⅞″.

FUCHSIA SILK MATKA

- Cut 24 squares 2⅞″ × 2⅞″.

TEAL RADIANCE SILK/COTTON BLEND

- Cut 18 squares 2⅞″ × 2⅞″.

TURQUOISE SILK DUPIONI

- Cut 12 squares 2⅞″ × 2⅞″.

Note: Add the scraps from the previous cuts of silk matka, Radiance silk/cotton blend, and silk dupioni randomly into the textile scraps mix for the smaller squares that follow.

SCRAPS

- Cut 116 squares 1⅝″ × 1⅝″.

Construction

If you do *not* have dividend units, construct half-square triangle units as instructed below.

LARGER HALF-SQUARE TRIANGLE UNITS

1. Draw a diagonal line from corner to corner on the wrong sides of 12 scrap 2⅞″ squares.

2. Pair these squares with 12 fuchsia matka squares, right sides together.

3. Sew a scant ¼″ seam on either side of each drawn line. Cut on the drawn lines. Each pairing yields 2 half-square triangle units measuring 2½″ × 2½″. Press the seams in one direction. There will be 24 scrap/fuchsia units.

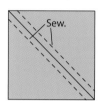 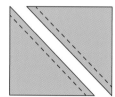

Half-square triangle units

4. Following the same process, construct 24 units with 12 fuchsia squares and 12 teal squares.

5. Construct 12 units with 6 teal and 6 turquoise squares.

6. Construct 12 units with 6 turquoise and 6 scrap squares. You will have a total of 72 larger half-square triangle units.

SMALLER HALF-SQUARE TRIANGLE UNITS

1. Randomly select 57 pairings of the 1⅝″ × 1⅝″ squares.

2. Construct 116 half-square triangle units as instructed above.

Assembly

1. Lay out the center panel by arranging the larger units into 6 rows of 12 units each. Control the color placement to create the chevron effect.

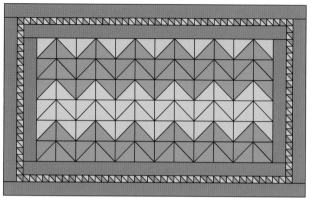

Bolster assembly

2. Sew the units in each row together. Press the rows in alternating directions.

3. Join the rows together. The center will measure 12½″ × 24½″.

4. Add the 2″ × 12½″ wool flannel strips to the sides of the center panel. Press the seams open.

5. Add the 2″ × 27½″ wool flannel strips to the top and bottom. Press the seams open.

6. Sew 2 rows of 20 smaller half-square triangle units each. Add a row to each side of the center. Press the seams toward the wool strips.

7. Sew 2 rows of 38 smaller half-square triangle units each. Add the rows to the top and bottom of the center. Press the seams toward the wool strips.

8. Add the remaining wool border strips. Sew the 17″ strips to the sides and then the 32″ strips to the top and bottom.

9. The project front should measure 20″ × 32″.

Finishing

The bolster can be finished with a simple knife-edge detail. To make it easier to insert the pillow form and to also create a flange detail at the outer edge, we finished it with a panel construction.

TIP • To give the bolster a slightly more decorative appearance, I did four lines of stitching approximately ¼″ apart on one of the chevrons on the top panel.

1. Finish one *short* edge of each of the 20″ × 22″ backing panels by turning under a ½″ hem and topstitching.

2. Place both back panels with right sides down on the right side of the bolster front panel. Align the raw edges of all 3 panels. The back panels will overlap each other by approximately 4″.

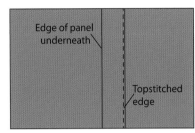

Back

3. Stitch around the entire outside edge. Turn the bolster right side out through the opening of the back panels. Press.

4. Pin or baste the overlapping back panels in place. Stitch in the ditch, through all the thicknesses, around the center panel *and* around the pieced inner border. This will create a flange. Insert the pillow form and enjoy!

Flange

Stitch in the ditch.

Dividends Table Topper

Finished block: *6″ × 6″*

Finished table topper: *42⅜″ × 42⅜″*

The *Dividends Table Topper* also uses both sizes of the dividend half-square triangle units. The distinction in this project is that the units are sewn into blocks and *then* set into the top. This was also a quilting experiment: The silk/cotton blend fabric, called Radiance, is amazing when quilted—I wanted to showcase what this fabric could do. The shine and the depth of color it lends to a project are wonderful.

Read Exploring New Textiles: Eclectic Fabric Guidelines (page 6) before beginning.

Note: Interface all the silk dupioni before cutting. Also test any other loose weaves to determine whether they would benefit from interfacing before you begin.

Materials

Dividend units: 64 smaller dividend half-square triangle units for center block *and* 108 larger dividend half-square triangle units for Nine-Patch blocks

Fuchsia Radiance silk/cotton blend: ¼ yard for alternate squares

Green Radiance silk/cotton blend: ½ yard for alternate squares

Teal Radiance silk/cotton blend: ⅝ yard for setting triangles

Brown wool flannel (54″–60″ wide): ½ yard for outer border

Backing: 2¾ yards

Binding: ½ yard

Batting: 50″ × 50″

If you are constructing the half-square triangle units and *not* using dividend half-square triangle units, you will also need these materials:

Scraps: Approximately 1 yard *total* of mixed eclectic textile scraps, such as silk dupioni, silk matka, silk/cotton blends, batiks, and mixed cottons

Cutting

DIVIDEND UNITS

• Trim 64 smaller dividend units to 1¼″ × 1¼″.

• Trim 108 larger dividend units to 2½″ × 2½″.

FUCHSIA RADIANCE SILK/COTTON BLEND

• Cut 4 squares 6½″ × 6½″.

GREEN RADIANCE SILK/COTTON BLEND

• Cut 8 squares 6½″ × 6½″.

TEAL RADIANCE SILK/COTTON BLEND

• Cut 2 squares 16″ × 16″; cut in half diagonally.

BROWN WOOL FLANNEL

• Cut 4 strips 3¾″ × 18″.

• Cut 4 strips 3¾″ × 21″.

BINDING

• Cut 5 strips 2½″ × width of fabric.

Note: Follow the remaining cutting instructions only if you are not using dividends from previous projects.

SCRAPS

• Cut 108 squares 2⅞″ × 2⅞″.

• Cut 64 squares 1⅝″ × 1⅝″.

Construction

If you do *not* have dividend units, construct half-square triangle units as instructed below.

HALF-SQUARE TRIANGLE UNITS

1. Draw a diagonal line from corner to corner on the wrong sides of 54 scrap 2⅞″ squares.

2. Randomly pair these squares with the 54 remaining scrap 2⅞″ squares, right sides together.

3. Sew a scant ¼″ seam on either side of each drawn line. Cut on the drawn lines. Each pairing yields 2 half-square triangle units measuring 2½″ × 2½″. Press the seams in one direction. There will be 108 larger half-square triangle units.

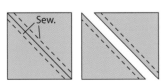

Half-square triangle units

4. Following the same process, construct 64 smaller half-square triangle units with the 1⅝″ scrap squares. These units will measure 1¼″ × 1¼″.

NINE-PATCH BLOCKS

1. Sew 9 of the larger half-square triangle units into 3 rows of 3 units each. Press the rows in alternate directions.

2. Sew the rows together. Press. Make 12 Nine-Patch blocks measuring 6½″ × 6½″. They will finish at 6″ × 6″.

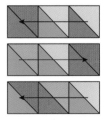

Nine-Patch rows

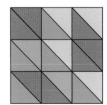

Nine-Patch block

CENTER BLOCK

1. Sew the 64 smaller half-square triangle units into 8 rows of 8 units each. Press the rows in alternate directions.

2. Sew the rows together. This center block will measure 6½″ × 6½″.

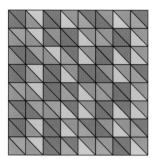

Center block

Assembly

1. Following the quilt center assembly diagram, arrange the Nine-Patch blocks, the center block, and the 6½″ fuchsia and green squares into 5 rows. Sew the blocks into rows. Press the rows in alternate directions.

2. Sew the rows together. The center will measure 30½″ × 30½″.

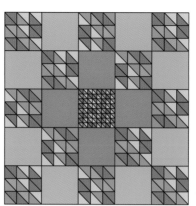

Quilt center assembly

Note: *The setting triangles for this project were designed using the teal Radiance fabric to showcase the quilting. They are large and open, leaving lots of room for the quilter to play! I also wanted the points of the center piecing to extend to the outer edge. That meant designing a pieced setting triangle. It's a little more of a challenge but opens up a world of design possibilities.*

3. Sew an 18″ wool flannel strip to each of the 4 teal Radiance setting triangles along one short side. Press the seam open.

4. Add the 21″ wool flannel strips to the 4 setting triangles along their other short sides. Press open. The edges of the outer border strips will extend beyond the edges of the setting triangle.

5. Following the diagonal cut edge of the setting triangle, trim the border strips.

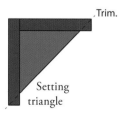

6. Sew the pieced setting triangles to the quilt center. Press toward the setting triangles.

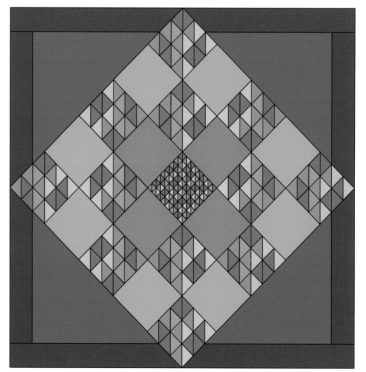

Quilt assembly

Finishing

1. Layer, baste, and quilt as desired.

2. Add binding (page 16).

Photo by Sean Henderson

About the Author

LYNN SCHMITT has worked in a design capacity for her entire professional life. She entered the design world as a fine arts student, ultimately graduating with a bachelor of fine arts in interior design. She then continued as an interior designer, specializing in commercial interiors for more than 30 years.

Lynn now colors outside the lines as the owner of A Different Box of Crayons, which officially launched in 2010. She has worked with and designed quilts for more than twelve years. Through A Different Box of Crayons, Lynn designs patterns and kits for the adventurous quilter using new techniques and an eclectic mix of cotton and alternative textiles. Her work has frequently been featured in *American Patchwork & Quilting* and *Quilts and More* magazines. She has had several projects published in Need'l Love quilt books.

Initially, Lynn's most popular projects focused on whimsical approaches to graphic imagery in quilts. Her current focus is on secondary patterning, color, texture, and eclectic textiles enhanced with wool appliqué. She

believes that with a little understanding of how to handle and sew with eclectic textiles, quilters need not be limited to just cotton fabric in their projects. Her Eclectic Bundles afford quilters access to silk matka, raw silk, silk dupioni, both hand-dyed and woven wools, linen, home decor textiles, and all scales and themes of cotton. In this book, Lynn illustrates how they can be beautifully brought together to dance in a single project. Truly a new "box of crayons" with which quilters of all ages and experience levels can learn to color!

FOLLOW LYNN ON SOCIAL MEDIA:

Website: adifferentboxofcrayons.com

(Visit A Different Box of Crayons at its new home in Glen Ellyn, Illinois, at 439 Pennsylvania Avenue, and experience firsthand the mix of color and texture that eclectics can create in your projects!)

Blog: myboxofcrayons.blog

Facebook: /adifferentboxofcrayons

Instagram: @adifferentboxofcrayons

Want even more creative content?

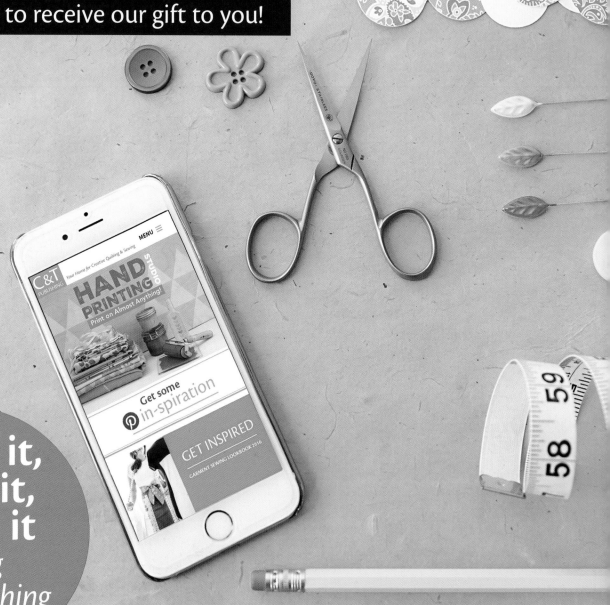

Make it, snap it, share it *using #ctpublishing*